Matthew Champagne

Survey Experts recommend *The Survey Playbook*

"I wish I had this book ten years ago! Anyone who is doing surveys must buy it today. The What, Where, Why, How, When section is worth the price of the book 20X over."

- JIM SELLNER, PH.D. AUTHOR OF LEADERSHIP FOR EINSTEINS: HOW SMART LEADERS BRING OUT THE GENIUS IN PEOPLE

"In the world of Big Data, KPI's, NPS, Business Intelligence, we all know the value of getting great feedback from our customers. However, getting that feedback is a challenging and intimidating process for most of us. *The Survey Playbook* is a sound, how-to guide for drawing out the results you want when using surveys. Doc Champagne's writing style is direct, professional and concise. Read this book before you ever do a survey."

- ROBERT ROSSI, M.S., MBA. SENIOR BUSINESS ANALYST, JLL

"I teach research methods and have developed survey instruments for many organizations and am impressed at the quality and accuracy of the advice and instruction given in *The Survey Playbook*. I enthusiastically recommend it."

- JEFFREY NICHOLAS, PH.D. ASSOCIATE PROFESSOR OF PSYCHOLOGY, BRIDGEWATER STATE COLLEGE

"There are ridiculously expensive workshops that are far less informative and useful than this easy-to-read gem. I'll be highly recommending this book to the many professionals I know involved in assessment."

- STEPHEN SCHEPMAN, PH.D., MBA. PROFESSOR OF PSYCHOLOGY, CENTRAL WASHINGTON UNIVERSITY

Practitioners praise *The Survey Playbook*

"Every organization should invest in this book before sending surveys."

"Extremely practical. It's filled with real examples and practical solutions. I now have a reference book to use when creating my next evaluation survey."

"Fantastic Resource. My surveys are getting rave reviews and a much higher completion rate."

"This book is entirely different! It takes a checklist approach in giving you the advice the author has learned over a career of 5,000 surveys."

"The format is so short and digestible that I read the entire book in about an hour, but now I'll go back and use the advice in every survey I do from now on."

"I learned exactly what I wanted to learn."

"If you want to know about surveys, this is a guy to follow."

"Easy to read and put into practice - thanks, Doc!"

"Extremely helpful. I use it more frequently than any other guide on survey and assessment tools. I highly recommend it."

More Practitioners praise *The Survey Playbook*

"Best book on surveys I've ever read."

"Excellent book with very practical tips on creating surveys."

"Make sure you sign up for Dr. Champagne's news. The tips sent allow me to continuously check survey quality."

"Best compendium of practical ideas backed by experience and research out there."

"Excellent book that you can digest in one or two sittings and refer to as needed when creating surveys."

"A short but practical book with lot of useful information that help right away."

"A must read for anyone planning to do a survey."

"Filled with succinct, practical advice, not at all academic or esoteric."

"Love it!! Clear, concise - and it works!"

"A practical set of dos and don'ts that I can immediately apply to the surveys I've been developing."

THE SURVEY PLAYBOOK

The Only Survey Guide You'll Ever Need

THE SURVEY PLAYBOOK
Volume 1: How to create the perfect survey

ISBN: 1499202164
ISBN-13: 978-1499202168

Cover and print book design by Greg Cosgrove

Matthew V. Champagne, Ph.D.

THE SURVEY PLAYBOOK

The Only Survey Guide You'll Ever Need

Volume 1: How to create the perfect survey

CONTENTS

CONTENTS

NEED IMMEDIATE HELP?

No time to read a book because you need to create that survey or evaluation form today? Need another pair of eyes to review your survey before it launches tomorrow? Write me and I'll help as quickly as possible! **champagne@EmbeddedAssessments.com**

NO, I'M GOOD...

No emergency? Whew! Then take time to join our community of survey experts and survey practitioners, enroll in some courses and learn much more at: **http://MatthewChampagne.com**

INTRODUCTION

My mission is to rid the world of annoying and poorly created surveys.

EVERYONE HAS THE SAME QUESTIONS

For more than two decades I have been asked the same questions hundreds of times by people across every type of organization:

- How do we increase our response rates?
- What is a "good" response rate?
- Are we asking the "right" questions?
- Is our survey too long?
- What are the best incentives?
- How do we stop spending so much on incentives?
- Why are our survey results ambiguous and not interpretable?
- Why don't our customers provide useful/actionable comments?
- People have survey fatigue - how often should we give surveys?
- No one fills out surveys anymore – what options do we have?

Whenever someone says that their surveys are not getting useful results or have low return rates or are too costly, it invariably means they are using ineffective survey practices. Fortunately, there are research-based answers to all these questions and practical solutions that can be applied in every situation.

Until now, the real problems were wasting time searching for all the right answers, and paying enormous consultant fees for unique answers to what are actually very common issues. This book solves these problems by providing a comprehensive checklist of every error that can be made in constructing a survey. Once you have read this book you will know everything I have taught hundreds of organizations about creating the best possible surveys. By comparing your existing surveys against this checklist you will see the gap that must be bridged to have an accurate and useful survey.

WHO IS THIS BOOK FOR?
There is a need for more accurate, meaningful and actionable survey results in every organization that gathers feedback through online surveys and paper forms. This book will be a valuable service to many. Are you:

- Tasked with creating a survey for customers, students, members, employees, alumni, or prospects?
- A do-it-yourself'er using any of the 90+ existing web-based online survey tools?
- An Evaluation Committee member responsible for improving your existing course evaluation forms?
- A tradeshow organizer gathering feedback from exhibitors and attendees?
- A College Administrator tasked with interpreting and acting on faculty evaluation results?
- A Customer Retention Specialist or otherwise dedicated to engaging and keeping customers?
- A Director of Training at your learning organization responsible for instructor evaluations?
- A Marketing Researcher who has heard conflicting messages about the usefulness of surveys?
- Someone using web-based or paper-based surveys for accreditation and evaluation purposes?
- Someone who gets annoyed when asked to waste time on a poorly constructed survey?

The solutions in this book have been successfully applied at hundreds of colleges and universities, learning organizations, service providers, and trade shows; as well as for surveys of church membership, fund-raising drives, elementary and secondary schools, military training evaluations, political polling, high school sports official ratings, and online focus groups. Any situation where timely and interpretable feedback can improve products and services will benefit from the theory-based and practical advice found in **The Survey Playbook**.

WHY ARE YOU WRITING THIS BOOK?

Since 1998, people have asked me for "best practices" and for names of organizations who are implementing surveys in a way that works and can be mimicked. But I want your school, organization, program or department to be the "best practice." I want your surveys to yield clear and informative results that others want to emulate. I want you to be the one that others look to as a model for their own surveys. To be that model, simply read this book and put the ideas into practice.

To be honest, I am also a bit fatigued. I continue to review and critique dozens of surveys every month, highlighting the same errors and offering the same advice. I thought it now time to codify these errors into a useful checklist that anyone can apply to their organization. By applying the checklist and advice in this book, you will have a robust, accurate and meaningful survey. Reading this book will save you time that can then be spent on the more critical tasks of interpreting and acting on your data.

BUT WHY ARE YOU GIVING AWAY THIS VALUABLE INFORMATION?

My mission has long been to rid the world of poorly conducted surveys that annoy customers and misinform organizations. No one intentionally creates a survey with misleading questions or one that will yield bad data. Survey makers are simply not trained and thus rely on gut feelings, conventional wisdom, and what they have seen others do. Yes, anyone can be a teacher or a coach, but not everyone does it well. The same is true of surveys – we have the tools so that anyone can create a survey but no one would vouch that the surveys we all receive on a weekly basis are high quality.

To rid the world of poor quality surveys we cannot solve problems one organization at a time but rather must widely share the secrets for creating the most useful and informative surveys possible to as many people as possible. So please, pass what you have learned on to others and spread the word!

WHAT IS WRONG WITH OUR SURVEYS?

When was the last time you said:

- "Oh boy, another survey in my inbox that I can't wait to fill out!"
- "I'm sure my valuable time is better spent filling out this survey than doing other tasks today."
- "I'm sure the people reading my answers will let me know how my feedback made a difference."
- "That survey was so well written that I'm sure they will understand my exact thoughts and feelings."

For many years I have given talks entitled "Surveys R.I.P." and "Surveys: why do we hurt the ones we love?" It was not always this way – years ago we used to get 50% response rates on unsolicited web-based surveys! The practice was rare and novel and people responded. But with the explosion of free and inexpensive do-it-yourself web survey tools and the rush to convert paper-based surveys to web-based surveys, receiving an email invitation to fill out a survey went from novel to burdensome to just plain annoying. The quality of surveys plummeted as these tools allowed anyone to easily create a survey, even those who knew little about how questions should be constructed.

For years we tried correcting the worst features of the typical survey and then rebranded it. Some focused on fixing the burdensome length of the survey and renamed it a "micro-survey" or "bitesize survey." The Net Promoter Score, utterly ubiquitous in the corporate world, eliminated the possibility of poorly constructed items by having just a single question. For others, the word "survey" had such negative connotations that they simply abandoned the technique. Many market researchers concede that surveys may play a limited role but have moved on to more interesting techniques like neuromarketing, social media analytics, and facial analysis for gathering customer feedback.

I also had avoided the word "survey" for many years, considering it to have too much baggage, and opted instead for the term **Embedded Assessment**^{TM} to describe a survey process that employs a set of principles that work. That is, *Embedded Assessment*^{TM} is constructing and delivering a survey and analyzing the results in the most ideal manner possible. But it still uses a survey! Since we cannot get rid of surveys, let's create them correctly, gather high numbers of responses and generate meaningful results, yes?

HOW DO YOU CREATE A GOOD SURVEY?
If we had unlimited time and resources we would sit down with each student in a class and ask specific questions about how they learn best and dig deep to learn what obstacles to learning existed. We would ask each trade show attendee to explain what they thought about each event and explain how each presenter captured their attention. We would ask each customer detailed questions about their recent visit or travel and systematically clarify each response until we were confident we understood their perceptions.

But we don't and we can't, so we create a survey instead. The survey (aka: bubble sheet, evaluation form) is meant to be a proxy for this detailed interview. But it is difficult to clarify answers or expand on areas of interest as they are being written. On a web-based survey we cannot hear when respondents pause and say "huh?" As soon as respondents pause, we have lost them.

We must instead produce a set of items and instructions that are so clear and unambiguous and compelling that the respondents' answers are interpreted exactly as they were intended. This almost never happens. For most surveys, there is a large gap between the respondent's perceptions and our interpretation of these perceptions. By applying the advice and checklist in this book that gap will be significantly narrowed and you will confidently know that you understood the respondents' thoughts and perceptions.

THE TYPICAL SURVEY
Here is a typical unspoken exchange that occurs when people fill out your surveys. Does this sound familiar?

Dear Member....	Gee, that's a warm fuzzy. Don't even know my name?
This survey takes 5 minutes to complete	Sure, doesn't every survey say this?
Q1: What do you think about this?...	The answer I want isn't here, so I'll leave this blank.
Q2: What is best about that?...	I don't understand, so I'll choose N/A
Q3: Why do you think this about that?...	There is no comment box. I guess they don't want my opinion.
Click "NEXT" to go to more questions...	Why can't they put all the questions on one page? I'm getting carpal tunnel!
What degrees have you earned?	Really? This isn't in your records?
You are 7% complete. Click "NEXT"...	#&%$@! I'm done. [Close browser]

People do not want to fill out surveys and do not provide useful responses because the survey content and process violates basic principles of human thought and behavior. In short, these surveys annoy and frustrate people and make them reconsider why they should spend time on the activity.

The key to success, therefore, is to ensure that the content, delivery, and process of your survey are consistent with psychological principles. That's it. That's the secret.

Twenty years of empirical research, data-gathering, conversations, and problem-solving for more than 500 organizations can be distilled into just *Nine Principles* of human thought and behavior that are applicable to surveys. By applying these *Nine Principles* to your survey construction and delivery, you will ensure that you are gathering accurate and actionable information. Future volumes of **THE SURVEY PLAYBOOK** series will explain each of these principles with real-life practical examples. Most of these principles can be incorporated quickly. And cost nothing.

THE NINE PRINCIPLES
Most gratifying to me is when someone says "did you make that survey? That was a GOOD survey!" When asked to explain, these respondents may say that the items were clear or complete or that they felt they were able to speak their mind, but usually they do not know all the reasons why it felt like a good survey. The true answer as to why they say it "feels good" is because the survey was constructed in a way consistent with psychological principles. A survey is annoying when it is constructed in a way that ignores these principles. There are just nine of these Principles and applying them is the difference between a great survey and an annoying one. Here they are: the who, what, where, when, why and how of the *Nine Principles* as they apply to surveys:

Nine Principles of Embedded Assessment™

WHY	1. Defining the Purpose and the Roles
WHAT	2. Improving the Content
WHEN	3. Timing and Frequency
WHO	4. Participation and Ownership
HOW	5. Closing the Loop
	6. Use of Incentives
	7. Training the Respondents
	8. Reporting
WHERE	9. Mode of Delivery
RESULTS	Response Rate, Engagement, Loyalty, Success

These *Nine Principles* have been explained in a series of publications from 1998 to 2013 but will be distilled into an easy-to-use set of Lessons in **THE SURVEY PLAYBOOK** series. This first volume you are reading is all about *Principle #2*, creating accurate, useful, and meaningful <u>content</u> in your surveys.

Since 1998, hundreds of learning organizations, service providers, colleges, and individuals have applied the *Nine Principles* and reported these successes:

1. Engaged their audience so that they <u>wanted</u> to provide feedback
2. Extracted <u>accurate</u> information from respondent feedback
3. Gathered <u>meaningful</u> feedback to make good organizational decisions
4. Rapidly <u>improved</u> their products and services, or their teaching and learning
5. Removed survey fatigue for their team and their respondents
6. Reduced budgets for lotteries and giveaways to $0
7. Gathered timely information to exceed customer expectations
8. Generally, made the world a better place (by eliminating bad surveys that fill our inboxes!)

WHY START WITH CONTENT?
We begin with Principle #2, *Improving the Content*, because it is relevant to every survey for every purpose and organization. Year after year in our annual survey of Higher Education, the second most popular concern (after response rate) is content: issues about the reliability, validity, clarity, representativeness, and relevance of the survey items. In other words, "are we asking the right questions in the right way?"

The importance of Improving the Content is recognized by companies that create do-it-yourself web-based survey tools and they address this need by offering their users access (for a fee) to survey experts who can assist in creating better content. The contradiction is that these web-based tools have default features and options that lead users to make bad choices in their survey construction. We will talk about some of these features and options to avoid in the upcoming lessons. This will allow you to use these tools but do so without harming the relationship between you and your respondents.

A NOTE ABOUT RESPONSE RATES

In the *Nine Principles*, having high return rates is not a Principle. It is the result of successful <u>application</u> of the Principles. It is relatively simple to predict the approximate return rate of a survey by examining how many of the *Nine Principles* have been applied. If all *Nine Principles* are satisfied it is almost certain that every individual who had something meaningful to say has responded to the survey. If none of the *Nine Principles* are satisfied, it is certain that your response rate is unacceptable and your results are meaningless. As each Principle is applied, the response rate increases. The same can be said about the engagement and loyalty of your respondents and the success of your survey efforts. I will point out these positive outcomes in each Lesson.

A NOTE ABOUT CLOSING THE LOOP *(Principle #5)*

"Closing the loop" is acknowledging the input from respondents and letting them know how you are taking action to address their specific concerns. When you ask someone to fill out a survey you are not only asking for their valuable time but you are setting the expectation that their feedback will be used and that it makes a difference. Closing the loop is NOT an auto-generated email message that says "thank you" or "your responses will help us improve our products and services." Rather it is feedback to the feedback, explaining to respondents how their specific ratings and comments can be acted upon and how they compare to others. We will describe Principle 5 in detail and provide many useful examples in an upcoming volume in this series. In the meantime, you will see the concept mentioned several times in passing in this volume.

HOW TO READ THIS BOOK

From seminars and workshops we have found that most readers digest this book in one of three ways:

1. Read all 25 lessons pausing after each to compare your own surveys with the advice presented.

2. Skip to those lessons that are of the most consequence and meaning to you and your team.

3. Read only the takeaway point of each lesson to determine if your surveys already heed this advice.

However you wish to read this book, it is time to rid the world of poorly created surveys that annoy customers and misinform organizations. Each lesson concludes with a TAKEAWAY that summarizes the lesson and a HOMEWORK assignment (because who doesn't love homework?), which are tips for spreading the word and to help end these annoying survey practices. Ready? Let's begin...

PART ONE

ADVICE FOR ITEMS AND QUESTION STRUCTURE

Lesson #1: Asking questions that you do not intend to change

The point of gathering feedback is to accurately hear what customers are saying, and then <u>act</u> on their responses. It does no good – in fact, it does more harm – to ask for opinions about topics that you have no intention of changing. Here are a few questions regarding logistics that you have likely seen on surveys given at trade shows, meetings, and training events:

- Was the room warm enough?
- Did you like the location for our reunion?
- Was there enough room in the Vendor Showcase?
- Was the classroom too small?
- Was our lobby bright enough?
- Would you prefer the event to run 3 days or 4 days?
- Is our location convenient?

In many cases, the location, environment, and logistics are fixed and cannot be altered. Events held in a certain city or hotel or classroom may well be held there again for the next event, regardless of the feedback received from attendees. When things are not changed, this will be interpreted by some attendees that you are not listening to what they say. You actually <u>are</u> listening, but simply cannot change those things in the way they have asked. Worse yet, many respondents will be aware of this and then wonder why you are wasting their time asking such questions.

This can also occur on training evaluation forms. If the course content is fixed, such as for certification programs, and there can be no variation in the material presented, then you should avoid asking questions that would lead students to believe that their input will be the basis for a decision to modify that content.

Takeaway: Re-read each item on your survey and ask yourself, "if a majority of respondents disagreed or indicated that a change should be made, CAN a change be made?" If not, then remove that item from your survey.

Homework (how to spread the word!): Next time you receive a survey, note any items that ask for an opinion on issues or processes that you know to be fixed or unlikely to be changed regardless of anyone's feedback. Leave those items blank and let the survey maker know that those items should be removed from the survey.

Lesson #2: Asking questions for which you already know the answers

This is a costly error to make as it often damages the relationship with your respondents. Here is an excerpt from a survey a colleague of mine received [her reaction shown in brackets]:

- **Dear Alumna/Alumnus:** *[Gee, that's a warm fuzzy. You don't even know my name?]*
- **Choose one: Male/Female** *[Uh, I went to your school for 4 years and you don't know the answer?]*
- **Select highest Degree Earned from the dropdown list:** *[This information isn't in your records?]*

Obviously my colleague never finished this survey and it left her with a poor impression of her alma mater. Another friend showed me an email he received from an auto dealership at which he had purchased a vehicle. Buried within the logos and images and marketing filler of the email was a request to fill out a survey. Clicking on the survey link, the first three questions were:

- *Enter your LAST name:*
- *Enter your FIRST name:*
- *Enter your email address:*

My friend's obvious questions were:

1. How do they not know my email address when they emailed me the survey request?
2. How come they don't know my name when I just bought a $35,000 vehicle from them?

My question would be:

3. Why would any customer fill out a survey that was so impersonal?

Of course this survey was generated from the VIN number of the new vehicle rather than by name or email of the customer, but a little effort would have produced a response from my friend instead of an immediate trip to the delete folder. For the tiny proportion of customers that bothered to type in their name and email, do you think they are now in the mood to give the dealership high ratings and positive comments?

I am often struck by the impersonal questions and unwelcoming tone of Alumni Surveys and Membership Surveys. At minimum, the full name and proper salutation of the respondent should be displayed on the online or paper form. Demographic, historical, and "obvious" information about the respondent should only be asked if it is made clear that you are only asking because you are uncertain if the records are up-to-date. For example:

"Do you still live at [870 McChesney Avenue] and is [888-555-1212] still the best number to reach you? If not, please edit these fields in the box below."

Takeaway: Treat others as you would want to be treated. Do not expect your customers, members, or alumni to fill out a survey when you violate your relationship by treating them as a stranger and asking for information they would expect you to know.

Homework: Many organizations use third parties to do their surveys and may not be aware that they are insulting you. Rather than immediately deleting the survey, call or email the organization that sponsored the survey and tell them what you think of this poor practice.

Lesson #3: Double-barreled items

A double-barreled item is one that asks respondents to rate two different issues but allows for just one answer. It is one of the easiest errors to spot and remove, yet double-barreled items are often found on surveys. Here are four examples:

	Strongly Agree	Agree	Neutral	Disagree	Strongly Disagree
1. My instructor was organized and prompt	O	O	O	O	O
2. Course objectives were clearly stated at the start of class	O	O	O	O	O
3. The teller was friendly and courteous	O	O	O	O	O
4. My meal arrived quickly, correctly, and to temperature	O	O	O	O	O

The problem with #1 above is that the instructor may have promptly arrived to class but her presentation was not organized. Or the instructor was organized but happened to come to the training session late. If the respondent checks *Strongly Agree* than we have no problem interpreting: the instructor was both organized and prompt. The problem occurs if the respondent chooses *Neutral* or *Disagree*. Is the respondent saying that the instructor was organized but not prompt? Or vice versa? Or neither organized nor prompt? Answers to double-barreled questions cannot be clearly interpreted. If both parts of the question are important, it should be split into two questions.

At first glance, #2 above does not look like a double-barreled question. But what does a respondent choose if the course objectives were clearly stated yet not done so until the middle of class? The respondent may agree with one portion of the statement and disagree with another portion and choose *Neutral*. Or the respondent may conclude that being "clearly stated" is more important in this question and choose *Agree* even though the objectives were not stated until late in the class. Using this thought exercise, it really cannot be known for certain what respondents intend with their response. Survey makers have to decide what is most important and frame the statement with one purpose (e.g., "Course objectives were clearly stated." Or "Course objectives were provided at the start of class.")

#3 above looks like a double-barreled item, but this may be an acceptable question to use as any rating of agreement on this scale could be interpreted. Being "courteous" is also a "friendly" behavior. It is difficult to think of how a teller could be discourteous yet still be friendly. If a respondent disagrees with this statement it is safe to say that the teller was perceived as not demonstrating the good impression that was expected. Choosing *Neutral* causes us problems with the interpretation, but then again that choice should not have been offered in the first place (see Lesson #12).

How about #4 above? The dreaded triple-barreled question! Clearly, there is too much going on in this item. Guests that disagree with this statement could be saying that the meal took too long OR was incorrect OR was not hot enough, OR some combination and the survey maker won't know what the respondent disagreed with (unless it can be inferred from the comments).

Takeaway: Re-read each item on your survey and note any AND or OR words and ask yourself if a respondent could reasonable say YES to one portion of the statement and NO to another. If so, you have a double-barreled item that needs to be broken into two items or rephrased to gather answers or topics that are most important to you.

Homework: Easy assignment this time! Double-barreled items are simple to spot. Let the survey maker know that these items should be reworded so your responses can be clearly interpreted.

Lesson #4: Ambiguous, awkward, unanswerable and other "bad" items

This error is a catch-all category of problems that we will simply label "bad questions". These questions can be easily identified and removed by simply re-reading the survey from the perspective of the respondent. But since bad questions occur so frequently it appears that many survey makers simply do not take the time to read their own surveys. Bad questions include:

- Awkwardly written items with ambiguous or multiple meanings
- Items requiring respondents to strain their memory to recall the answer
- Items with unknown answers that force respondents to guess

Each of these bad questions not only yields questionable or uninterpretable results but also makes the respondent pause and ponder. We never want respondents to pause as that gives an opportunity to quit the survey. Ambiguous items are easy to spot by simply reading the stem as if you are the respondent and considering whether anyone could reasonably choose more than one answer. Here is an example:

1. Please indicate if you are concentrating on a degree or certificate program, or if you are simply taking one or two courses via the university's program.

After re-reading this item several times I think I may understand what they are asking but would a student be so patient? Would the student be able to differentiate between types of programs? Would they have yet decided whether they are "simply taking one or two courses" or if applying their coursework towards a degree? Here is another example, one that may be impossible for some to accurately answer:

2. *How many online courses have you taken in the past?*

Although some respondents might easily respond "zero" or "one or two," many of us would need time to dredge through our memories, thinking back to "the past" (is that recent past or dating back 15 or 20 years?). Does this question count only traditional college and high school courses or MOOCs and non-credit courses? What about intensive web-based events – surely those must count for something if the survey maker is trying to gauge experience, right? Once the respondent pauses to interpret the question, you risk losing their answer or gathering uninterpretable responses.

In both of these cases the best solution is to think through the purpose of asking the question and determine the best way to express the question in words. Perhaps the purpose for #2 above is to make sure respondents have a minimal level of experience with online courses, in which case you can explain in the question that an exact number of courses is not really necessary.

Takeaway: Bad questions are easily spotted by your customers, so take the time to review your own survey. Re-read each item on your survey and ask yourself whether all respondents can answer it quickly, accurately, and effortlessly. If the answer is no, then modify or eliminate that item.

Homework: When in doubt, fill in a comment box on your survey to explain the ambiguity or your inability to determine what the survey maker is trying to ask. A responsive vendor would see your comment while the survey is in progress and may modify it or attempt to get your response by another means.

Lesson #5: Facet vs. global measures

Consider: Years ago employees at an organization were confidentially asked about their level of satisfaction with various facets of their job, such as the work environment, co-workers, responsibilities, and supervision. One employee rated every facet of the job as poor. The working conditions? Poor. The hours? Poor. The amount of support? Poor. After answering the lengthy list with the identical response, the consultant asked the final question about her OVERALL satisfaction with the company. Surprisingly, her answer was she was quite satisfied. "They allow me to talk on the phone with friends and family during business hours," she explained. The lesson: we should not assume that we can comprehensively identify every facet that goes into a human's decision.

This lesson about the lack of consistency between overall (global) satisfaction and our satisfaction with individual job facets was learned decades ago by I/O Psychologists but is often not put into practice in our surveys. A typical survey of a phone representative might ask multiple questions about the rep's knowledge, professionalism, friendliness, and courtesy, which are all trying to get at the core question of "would you want to be on the phone again with this person?" If the survey then asks the overall question of performance do we bother to note how similar the answers to the facet measures are to the global measure? If they differ then we have likely overlooked critical facets of the exchange between rep and customer.

Do we even ask the correct global measure? You may find very different answers to these three versions of the global question:
1. *Rate the overall performance of this representative.*
2. *Overall, were you satisfied with your experience with this representative?*
3. *Would you want this person to be the one to answer the next time you call?*

It is trendy for companies to simply ask the Net Promoter Score form of the global question: "On a scale from 0 to 10, would you recommend us to others?" Whether the response is a 6 (classified as a "detractor" that lowers your score), an 8 (called a "passive") or a 9 (called a "promoter" that raises your score), the question is WHY did they give that rating? We expect people to fill in the comment box and explain, but when they do not (which is often) what are we to make of these ratings if we have not asked about individual facets of the experience that may underlie this overall rating? (The Net Promoter Score is discussed in detail in the **Applications to Learning Organizations** chapter at the end of this volume).

In summary, organizations do not thoughtfully consider the facet vs. global distinction when:
1. the survey asks for ratings on a series of facets and assumes to have captured ALL critical facets;
2. the survey does not ask for any facets, relying instead on a global measure (e.g., the Net Promoter Score); and
3. analysis is not done between facet and global measures to determine their relationship.

It is important to determine the quantitative score of your customers' perceptions but just as important to know WHY they rated as they did. Failing to determine the critical facets of performance means that you are not learning all you can from your survey.

Takeaway: It is time well spent to consider the format of the overall (global) items on your survey and to compare the response on those items with individual facet items to see if they are correlated or inconsistent. Perhaps you are missing some critical items in your survey.

Homework: Have you ever finished a survey and wondered why an item was "missing" – some aspect or question that you had thought would be asked or that you thought was important? Be sure to fill in the comment box with "hey, how come you didn't ask me about XYZ?" Hopefully they'll take your advice and modify their survey.

Lesson #6: Gathering no prior input from respondents or direct stakeholders

Survey questions and categorizations should be revisited each administration and be guided by historical data and careful consideration. Two other resources to build useful and meaningful survey items are (1) your audience (respondents) and (2) those directly and most impacted by the results of the survey (direct stakeholders).

Respondents. Since you often already have a relationship with the respondents and have likely communicated in the past, asking these potential respondents for items that are of interest is a good practice when modifying a survey or formulating a new one. This step will also help to eliminate problems identified in other lessons including missing choices (Lesson #9), asking things you cannot change (Lesson #1), and asking too many questions (Lesson #16).

When creating a survey for a large audience of members, alumni, or customers, their input is helpful for items containing a list of choices such as:
- Which Webinar topics would be of most interest?
- Which product features are most useful?
- Which of the following locations do you prefer for our upcoming event? (If it makes a difference! See Lesson #1)

Rather than risk overlooking some reasonable choices, I reach out to folks that have responded to similar surveys in the past or to a subset of my current list of respondents. I gather comprehensive replies from this informal focus group from open-ended questions in an email (e.g., "Which locations would you absolutely NOT wish to attend?") and then use those answers to form my questions to the larger audience.

This smaller group is told they are helping to guide the creation of a survey of a larger membership, thanked profusely, and given an interesting snippet of the results (see Principle Five: "closing the loop"). With just a small investment of time the final survey is more focused, actionable, and complete.

Direct Stakeholders. Although the respondents described above are certainly impacted by the results of a survey and are therefore considered "stakeholders," I describe those within an organization that are most impacted financially and otherwise by the survey results to be "direct stakeholders." This includes employees for an HR survey and faculty or trainers for a course evaluation. A survey need not be top-down or from an inflexible vendor form that omits some of the important questions (we will learn more about this in Lesson #24). Since the results of the survey will impact organizational decisions that affect employees, why not give them a voice as to what questions are asked.

NOTE: This is not the same as creating a "survey by committee," which almost always results in the worst possible survey and is the quickest way to sabotage your survey efforts. Asking direct stakeholders is not the same as asking each department in your organization to contribute questions, resulting in a multi-purpose, confusing, and lengthy survey. Rather, it is an information-gathering exercise to ensure that you are asking the most pertinent and useful questions.

Takeaway: Do not assume that you and your team know every important question that can be asked. Take time to leverage the minds of a few respondents and direct stakeholders to ensure that important and interesting questions and response choices have not been left behind.

Homework: It should be easy to spot surveys that are "created by committee" – they are lengthy, complex and annoying. But you should also keep an eye out for surveys that suffer from lack of input from those individuals who could have made the items more relevant. If you find missing choices and have to type a lot of comments to explain what you are trying to say then you likely have a survey that did not have sufficient input in the design.

Lesson #7: Stale items

Another irritating survey practice is failing to update and refresh your survey items from time to time. Sometimes it is just an oversight, such as Alumni Surveys or Employment Surveys where the possible choices for year of graduation or years of employment do not include the most recent year on the calendar. More often leaving stale items on the survey is a strategic choice by companies. Their argument is, yes, the question is rather outdated but we need to keep asking it so we can compare answers year over year. But is this necessary? Have you already learned all you can learn from previous responses to the question? Has not technology, the nature of your business, the people answering the survey, the environment or life changed so that the item should also change?

I understand the rationale for not wanting to change survey items every quarter or every year, which makes comparisons over time difficult to interpret, but many organizations take this approach to the extreme and keep irrelevant items or those that have been answered comprehensively in the past and are no longer needed. Yes perhaps some people still use AOL and Windows 95 but does that choice need to be kept on your drop down menu? What will you do with that data?

From our Introduction we learned that one of the *Nine Principles* is PURPOSE – consider <u>why</u> you are conducting the survey and what do you hope to achieve with the results. Perhaps questions you have asked about facets of life and work satisfaction, quality of products, location of meetings, or instructor qualities have already been addressed and answered and nothing new can be gained by asking the same questions to a different cohort of individuals.

The concern is that your respondents will identify these stale items and they will pause to consider why you are asking questions for which you already should have answers. Respondents who are willing to provide you feedback want to know that their responses made a difference and you violate this relationship when they perceive that nothing they say can make a contribution since the questions or choices are irrelevant or outdated.

Takeaway: You should revisit and refresh your surveys before every administration. Wholesale changes are usually not needed and are not advisable since you may want to compare answers to similar questions over time. But re-read each item and determine if knowing the answers will benefit your organization or if you are asking it just because it has been asked in the past.

Homework: Do you ever pause while filling out a survey and wonder why an item or choice was included? Do you question if it will make a difference whether you chose one response or another? If you feel that some of the questions on the survey are "stale" let the survey maker know by writing about it in a comment box. Perhaps they will take your advice and update their survey.

Lesson #8: The BEST questions to ask

"OK, Doc, so you've told us everything about what NOT to do in constructing items for a survey, but what ARE the very best questions to ask on my survey?"

Glad you asked! Here are three of my favorite questions:

1. "What is the one question that you did not get a chance to ask?"
Why it is a favorite: This question is typically found on training evaluation forms, student ratings of instructors, or post-hoc evaluations of meetings or presentations. It is most useful when prompted DURING the session as a pulse point question for discussion but is also helpful as a post-hoc question.

Educators know that there are always students who do not raise their hands during class and presenters know that lack of time often curtails questions at meetings and training sessions. Asking this question on the survey form leaves a positive impression on participants and usually generates the most unexpected and interesting points of view. If administered in midstream, those points can enrich the discussion and engage participants while the training or meeting is still in session. If administered post-hoc, selected answers can be later shared with all participants (aka "closing the loop," Principle Five). Responses to this question can be game-changers, sparking new ideas and innovations. More often the responses help us to see what gaps occurred during the training or presentation, and give us the opportunity to fill those gaps with follow up communication. Consider this question for any customer, employee or peer survey as well.

2. "Use the box below to clarify your answers: help us to understand WHY you gave those particular ratings."
Why it is a favorite: As we said earlier, the paper or web-based survey is a proxy for an interview. If we had unlimited resources we

would interview each customer face-to-face or by telephone, asking them to clarify each response until we were confident we understood their thoughts and feelings on the issue. Since we do not have unlimited resources we use a survey. BUT we must be sure that the survey is as close to an interview as possible and that means encouraging the respondent to express the meaning behind their responses. Of course we do not want to overdo it and ask "why?" after every item. That would be annoying. Rather, this prompt can occur after each facet or group of items related to a single criterion, or as a final question.

3. "Would you recommend this [product/service/company] to a friend or colleague?"

Why it is a favorite: There is a reason this question is so ubiquitous in organizations and has been called "the most important question." It can yield valuable results but ONLY if constructed and analyzed correctly. As I have argued elsewhere, the Net Promoter Score calculation is flawed and usually misleading because it ignores how humans make decisions. Instead, use my preferred structure for this question described in the **Applications to Learning Organizations** chapter at the end of this volume and ALWAYS ask respondents to clarify why they gave that particular rating.

Takeaway: Asking one or more of these questions in every survey will yield unexpected and interesting findings, provide actionable results, and help you better understand the perceptions of your customers.

Homework: The "recommend" question is found everywhere, but how often do you see the "one question you did not ask" item? Even if not prompted, be sure to fill in an open comment box with a question of your own and ask the survey maker to close the loop and provide you with an answer.

PART TWO

ADVICE FOR
RESPONSE SCALES

Lesson #9: Items with missing choices (i.e., don't insult me with "Other")

One frustrating situation for respondents is when they want to express their opinion on a question but the most exact answer is not offered. So they might waffle between two choices and pick the closest one. Or they might leave the item blank. Or they might fill in a comment box later in the survey to point out that you forgot to include the answer they wanted. In the paper-and-pencil world they might fill in a different answer in the margins or circle the area between choices. Regardless of their action you have failed to anticipate all reasonable responses and thus did not capture what your respondents were thinking and now your results may be misleading.

This error is compounded when asking questions about job title, occupation, market silo, and other characteristics about which people are very particular. You may lose respondents when you force them to choose *Other* as if their specific title or job classification is not important enough to include as an answer.

In one survey where I prompted college administrators to type in their job title, the result was 135 unique titles given by the 178 respondents! Should I have instead created a drop-down response scale box with 135 choices? Could I have anticipated 135 different answers? How many individuals would have left the item blank or been a bit annoyed if I included just a few broad choices (e.g., Director, Chair, Provost, Manager) and left them to fill in their important job title under *Other*?)

The lesson is that this error can occur even when you intentionally try to make the list of choices extremely long so as to offer every conceivable answer. The solution is to reconsider why you are asking the question and to think through how the data will be analyzed. Perhaps you do not need to code responses with a numeric value but instead can leave the responses open-ended.

You can use historical data, previous administrations of the survey, or input from your stakeholders (see Lesson #6) and others to best guide you to all reasonable choices. You should include an open-ended choice - just do not label it "Other!" Here is one good way to apply this lesson:

1. What is your job title? [open ended comment box]

2. In order to summarize all responses we also need to group all job titles into one of four specific categories. Choose the one category below that BEST describes the work you do:
   a. Partner
   b. Associate
   c. Counsel
   d. Administrative
   e. None of these categories fit me. The best category is really: [fill-in-blank]

The problem of omitting potential choices can be solved by carefully re-reading your survey and anticipating and including every reasonable response that could be given. If you are not certain and have no historical data to assist, then an open-ended choice may be best. Then use what you learn to compose a multiple choice item on your NEXT administration of the survey.

Takeaway: Be careful that your survey does not omit key choices that would be a reasonable answer to your respondents. Where possible, avoid annoying respondents by making them label their characteristics or choices as "other," as if it is so unusual that there exists no category for them.

Homework: Have you ever written in the margins or between the choices on a paper-based survey to more accurately reflect your response? But how do you convey a similar message on a web-based survey? Be sure to use the comment box to explain to the survey maker that the choice you wanted was not available so they can modify their content.

Lesson #10: Failing to define all choices

One of the most common bad practices and one that is rarely addressed is failing to give descriptors for every anchor on your response scale. Most surveys that use a Likert-type scale correctly anchor each of the 5 points, ranging from *Strongly Agree* to *Strongly Disagree*. The problem usually occurs when survey makers get creative or use 7- or 9-point scales, anchoring just the end points and perhaps the midpoint.

Rule #1 in Psychology is "people are different" and respondents have different perceptions as to what the undefined anchors mean. Survey makers violate Rule #1 and assume that everyone will interpret the scale in the same way and interpret the mental distance between the points to be of identical lengths, like this:

```
POOR |------------|-------------|-------------|-------------| TERRIFIC
       1           2             3             4             5
```

However, people do not interpret these scales the same. Different people may look at the scale above and judge the mental distance to look like this:

```
POOR |---|----X----------------------|----------------------| TERRIFIC
       1  2   3                        4                      5
```

The respondent in this example sees little difference between a rating of 1, 2, or 3 (all are pretty bad) and chooses a *3* to indicate that they are not happy. But the survey maker will misinterpret this rating thinking it to be about average, neither good nor bad, and assume the rater is not unhappy.

Another person may look at the same scale but internally judge the mental distance to look like this:

POOR |------------|-------------------|------------------**X**----| TERRIFIC
　　　1　　　　2　　　　　　3　　　　　**4** 5

This person rarely rates anyone or anything a *5*, reserving it for exceptional cases. Instead she chooses a *4* to say she was delighted with the service. The service provider is disappointed by a *4* (and maybe will not receive a raise because did not receive all *5s*!) and wonders what could be improved when, in fact, nothing needed improvement. The most egregious violator of Rule #1 is the ubiquitous "Net Promoter Score" (i.e., the "0 to 10 scale") described in detail in the **Applications to Learning Organizations** chapter later in this volume.

The solution is to thoughtfully choose descriptors for EVERY anchor. Each descriptor should have a clear and unambiguous meaning. This example is crystal clear and will lead to interpretable results:

1 = Definitely No
2 = Probably No
3 = Probably Yes
4 = Definitely Yes

Someone choosing a *3* is categorically different than someone choosing a *2* or a *4*. We will talk more about labels in the next Lesson, but for now just be sure that each anchor on your response scale is labeled and done so in a way that can reasonably only have one meaning. If you cannot think of meaningful descriptors for a 9-point scale then you should ask yourself whether you need 9 points or whether fewer anchors will do.

Takeaway: Keep Rule #1 in mind and do not leave any anchors on your response scale undefined. To do so invites respondents to interpret the points in different ways, leaving you with ambiguous and uninterpretable results.

Homework: The next time you fill out a survey with an un-anchored response scale, think about why you chose a particular rating and whether others may choose the same rating but for different reasons.

Lesson #11: Items mismatched with the response scale

Surveys often use the same response scale type for all questions, even when that response scale does not match all the items on the survey. Respondents will still fill out the survey but are left to try and interpret how the question fits the scale and in many cases it will be unclear what they intended. The most common error is using the ubiquitous 5-point Likert-type scale (*Strongly Agree* to *Strongly Disagree*) but framing the statements in terms of quality, frequency, or amount. The four examples below illustrate a distinct mismatch between the type of item and the type of response scale:

	Strongly Agree	Agree	Neutral	Disagree	Strongly Disagree
1. I attended sessions regularly	O	O	O	O	O
2. I took advantage of my instructor's office hours	O	O	O	O	O
3. The pace of the course was satisfactory	O	O	O	O	O
4. My experience with National Rental was excellent	O	O	O	O	O

Item #1 suggests frequency. The survey maker probably wants to know how often the respondent attends the sessions (e.g., never, once or twice, several times) but instead uses the word "regularly" and asks respondents to rate their level of agreement. This leaves the respondent's choice open to interpretation: if the respondent "disagrees," how many sessions did they attend? None? All but one? The meaning of "regular" will differ from person to person.

Item #2 is a Yes/No item or one that involves frequency. The survey maker has to decide what is important here — knowing whether respondents attended office hours at all, or how often. If a respondent "agrees" with the statement does that mean they attended one time or every week? Respondents who "disagree" may have attended as many times as others but it was their perception that they had not taken advantage of every opportunity.

The results of item #3 cannot be interpreted. If a respondent disagrees, we cannot know whether they are saying the pace of the course was too fast or too slow. No improvements can be made based on feedback where *Disagree* or *Strongly Disagree* is chosen.

Item #4 violates the neutral statement requirement. By using the qualifier "excellent," the results are difficult to interpret. Some respondents will often choose *Agree* as the highest possible rating – that is they agree that the experience was indeed excellent! Those interpreting the results (*Agree* is a 4 on a 5-point scale) will think they were not fully satisfied, but it is an artifact of a poorly designed item. Do not use qualifiers (e.g., great, outstanding) that will be redundant with the response scale.

Each item on your survey must be considered in terms of the response scale that fits the item. Is the question about PREFERENCE? If so, then a scale ranging from *Strongly Agree* to *Strongly Disagree* is appropriate. Is the question about comparisons? Speed or strength? Ease or difficulty? Amount? Each of these types of questions requires a different response scale. Here are three of the most common formats:

1. Question involves AGREEMENT? Try this 4-pt scale:
   ☐ Definitely Yes
   ☐ Probably Yes
   ☐ Probably No
   ☐ Definitely No

2. Question involves FREQUENCY? This may be appropriate:
    - ☐ Always
    - ☐ Often
    - ☐ Sometimes
    - ☐ Never

3. Question involves QUALITY? Try:
    - ☐ Excellent
    - ☐ Very Good
    - ☐ Good
    - ☐ Fair
    - ☐ Poor

Takeaway: Re-read each item on your survey and each possible answer on your survey, and ask yourself, "if a respondent chooses this answer, can I know for certain what they are trying to say?" If not, rewrite the item stem until each answer choice yields an unambiguous meaning.

Homework: Take note when you have to choose from a response scale choices that do not fit. If it leaves room for interpretation then clarify your response in any available comment box. Tell the survey maker that this is a common error and needs to be fixed.

Lesson #12: Unnecessary use of the neutral or opt-out options

There are several ways that survey makers can lose information with their survey. One way is by allowing respondents to skip questions for which they certainly hold an opinion. Surveys often contain options labeled *Not Applicable* or *Neither Agree nor Disagree* or *Neutral*. These choices are appropriate when respondents may not have the information or experience to answer. But they should be used strategically, not provided as an option for ALL items. Here are a few examples:

EXAMPLE 1:	**Excellent**	**Good**	**Fair**	**Poor**	**Not Applicable**
Overall, my experience at this store was:	O	O	O	O	O
EXAMPLE 2:	**Strongly Agree**	**Agree**	**Disagree**	**Strongly Disagree**	**N/A**
My instructor's communication style was effective.	O	O	O	O	O
EXAMPLE 3:	**Yes**	**No**	**Not Sure**		
I would recommend this business to my friends or colleagues.	O	O	O		

In each case above, the respondent has certainly had an experience and can provide some feedback. For #1, the individual <u>did</u> visit the store. She may not have bought anything and may not have stayed long, but she must have some opinion and that is what you are soliciting. Providing a *Not Applicable* option allows the respondent to prevent you from learning her opinion. The *Not Applicable* option may be fine for other categories, such as questions about customer service or the public restrooms, which the respondent may not have used.

In #2 above, all students in the training session listened to the instructor. And all students should have some opinion on the instructor's communication style. But some proportion of respondents will choose "N/A" since it is offered, and you will lose their information. The *N/A* option may be fine for questions about measures of performance that may not have been administered or course materials that may not have been distributed. All students should provide an opinion on characteristics of the instructor.

In #3, the *Not Sure* option may comprise a significant proportion of the respondents, providing you with little information except that they were not convinced. A much better alternative is to force respondents to make a choice but allow them to "lean" in one direction or the other, as in this variation:

I would recommend this business to my friends or colleagues.	Definitely Yes O	Probably Yes O	Probably No O	Definitely No O

Respondents can choose *Probably Yes* to indicate that they are not enthusiastic or do not plan to actively promote your business and that something has caused them to not choose *Definitely Yes*. Respondents can choose *Probably No* to not be a full rejection, that they have concerns or perhaps do not know enough information to recommend. Both provide far more information about their decisions than the response of "not sure" or a neutral point. This scale is also more interpretable than the ubiquitous Net Promoter Scale (see **Applications to Learning Organizations** chapter). In all cases you will want to review their comments to learn why they responded as they did.

Takeaway: Carefully review each item on your survey that contains a neutral option. Consider whether there could be a situation in which respondents will not have sufficient information or experience to answer. Those items and only those items should have a neutral option.

Homework: When filling out a survey, do you ever choose the neutral or not applicable option? Are you doing so because you truly have no opinion or you did not want to take the time to think through the question, or were you trying to say something else to the survey maker but the survey did not allow it?

Lesson #13: Losing Information by categorizing ordinal or interval data

In Lesson #12 we learned how survey makers can lose information through overuse of the opt-out option. Another way we can lose information on a survey is by turning ordinal or interval data into nominal data; that is taking good meaningful specific numbers and lumping into poorly defined categories.

We have all seen these types of questions on surveys:
- *How many years of experience do you have?*
- *How many trade shows have you attended?*

Each of these questions has specific, meaningful answers:
- *I have 13 years of experience*
- *I have attended 8 trade shows*

But the survey maker will never learn our specific answer because the survey forces us to choose among categories of answers, like this:

How many years of experience do you have?
- O   0-3 years
- O   4-6 years
- O   7-10 years
- O   More than 10 years

How many trade shows have you attended?
- O   0
- O   1-4
- O   5-8
- O   More than 8

Rather than learn the answer is "13 years", the survey maker only knows our answer is more than 10. Rather than learn the answer is "8 trade shows", the survey maker only knows our answer falls between 5 and 8.

We do not do this in everyday conversations – we would not respond to a question by saying "my batting average is between .300 and .325." We would say "my batting average is .316." If asked "how many scoops of ice cream do you want?" you would not say "between 1 and 4, please." You would say "2 scoops."

In the analysis, when we group numbers, all values within that group are treated as equal. This is fine if the data is truly categorical, such as male versus female. In this case we can accurately interpret the results: if females also have far more positive perceptions about an issue than males, we can act on these clear results.

The mistake is when we try to treat an interval-type measure like "experience" as if it were categorical. For the example above, our analysis of results would consider people with 4, 5, or 6 years of experience as identical but people with 7 years of experience as different from those with 6 years (they are in different categories). In my experience, the categories are rarely chosen based on historical data (i.e., there is something truly different about people that have 6 years vs. 7 years of experience), but rather just made up on the spot and not defensible (i.e., why not make the category 6-9 years or 7-11 years?) We will talk about choosing meaningful categories in the next lesson.

The result of these arbitrary categories is poor decisions made based on muddled results that mask what respondents are truly saying. The solution is to ask the question so that your respondent can provide the clear answer:

> **How many years of experience do you have? _____ years**
>
> **How many trade shows have you attended? _____**

You will soon discover interesting findings in your data that were previously hidden due to this loss of information artifact. Perhaps respondents with just 1 year of experience react differently to other items on your survey than those with 2 years of experience and you can act upon this information.

Consider this advice in terms of the *Nine Principles*: most people do not like to be lumped into a category. Some may take particular pride in their "18 years of experience" but now they have to choose "more than 10 years" and are lumped in with others having far less experience.

Takeaway: If you want to know what your customers are saying, do not lose specific information by forcing them to translate their actual answer into some arbitrary category. Instead prompt them to give specific answers that will give you specific and useful results. People do not usually like to be lumped into a category!

Homework: Next time you receive a survey, identify each loss-of-information artifact described above, and consider whether the survey maker will truly understand your answers on the survey when your specific quantitative response is lumped into an arbitrary range of numbers.

Lesson #14: How to choose meaningful categories for your questions

In Lesson #13 we learned that you can lose information on a survey by creating poorly defined categories. For example:

> **How many years of experience do you have?**
> O 0-3 years
> O 4-6 years
> O 7-10 years
> O More than 10 years

If the real answer from a respondent is "21 years," the survey maker will only learn that the respondent has "more than 10." We might also end up with too few respondents in a particular group, causing problems with interpretation. In the previous lesson we said that the solution is to simply ask the open-ended question: "How many years of experience do you have?" However, if you must categorize interval-level data, then the next best solution is to use categories that have meaning based on historical data or introspection. That is, in the analysis, all choices within the group are treated as equal, so can these age groups be defined so that there is more similarity <u>within</u> groups than <u>between</u> groups? In the above example, all people with more than 10 years experience are seen as "equal" in the analysis (all responses are coded as 4). Is this true? If not, can we break that group down into two or more meaningful categories?

Looking through historical data (e.g., past administrations of the same survey, membership records, other sources) you may find that the range of experience for your sample extends from 1 year to 29 years. Further, you discover that only a handful of people have more than 20 years of experience. Armed with this information, you might add a category and revise:

How many years of experience do you have?
○ 1-5 years
○ 6-10 years
○ 11-15 years
○ 16-20 years
○ More than 20 years

Thinking further, you realize that most of your participants must take a certification exam after 4 years and therefore there is something different about those with 5 years versus those with 4 years experience. You also discover in previous data collected that there are relatively few individuals with 14 to 20 years of experience and disproportionately more with 5 to 8 years of experience. Perhaps there is something different about those individuals who remain members beyond their 8th year or those with 14 or more years. You revise accordingly:

How many years of experience do you have?
○ 1-4 years
○ 5-8 years
○ 9-13 years
○ 14-20 years
○ More than 20 years

Now these groupings above are still not as clear cut as true categories such as "male" or "female," but the groups are more defensible following this introspection and the analysis will be more meaningful.

Takeaway: If you must use categories, then take the time to look at responses from previous surveys or other available data to thoughtfully consider the ranges of values to be included in each group. All respondents within that group are considered "equal" in the analysis so there should be less variability <u>within</u> a group than <u>between</u> groups.

Homework: Next time you receive a survey, consider whether the categories displayed appear thoughtfully constructed or created out of convenience. If you are forced to choose the "more than" category do you feel that your true response will not be accurately heard?

Lesson #15: Miscellaneous Errors: A final checklist

We have now covered all the major topics on creating good survey content and response scales, but there are still a few gaps to fill. Compare the five issues on the checklist below against your survey:

1. **Misuse of response scales.** Be sure that all reasonable answers to the questions are present and that each item matches its response scale. A few easy errors to spot include:
   - Gaps and overlaps – where the true response falls between two of the available choices or into two different choices. For example, choices are "3 to 5 years" and "5 to 8 years" of experience. Someone with "5 years" of experience could select either choice.
   - Overuse of drop down options – there is more chance of human error using drop downs, so use radio buttons wherever possible.
   - Misuse of radio buttons – some questions could reasonably have two or more answers and you will misinterpret responses if mistakenly offer a radio button format (allows one choice) instead of a checkbox format that allows multiple choices.

2. **Ambiguity of the neutral option.** In Lesson #12 we learned that *Not Applicable, Neither Agree nor Disagree,* and *Neutral* should be used strategically and not provided as an option for ALL items. In addition, take note that these phrases have different meanings and may be mismatched with the question. Survey makers use them interchangeably, relying on respondents to interpret however they wish, but this fuzziness often may cause some respondents to leave the item blank or to misinterpret your intention and thus leads to ambiguous results.

3. **Leading questions.** Anyone who has filled out a political party poll or survey has seen these. Of *course* you are supposed to circle YES for every item (and do not forget to include your $25 donation

to the candidate!). Everyone recognizes that political surveys are built on leading questions and that is ok because the survey maker is not interested in your answer as much as in your financial support. But there is no place for leading questions within a survey where you are truly trying to discover customer perceptions and attitudes.

I once reviewed a survey that was otherwise solid, but contained this item: "Would you choose to pay a higher fee to join a debt management company that works directly for you, or would you rather pay a lower fee to join a company whose principal source of income is from the credit card companies to whom you are indebted?" Of course they want you to say yes (once you have figured out that lengthy question!) but now the survey is guilty of mixing purposes (see Lesson #19) and respondents start to question the intent of the survey and wonder whether the company is truly interested in their responses or using them to satisfy another agenda.

4. **Too many items.** We will discuss this topic in much more detail in upcoming lessons, but for the purpose of this checklist be sure that your survey focuses on a single purpose, without redundant items, with excellent prompts for encouraging comments, without using the NEXT button, and done in a way that demonstrates you are interested in your respondents' opinions. If so, then you have the correct number of items no matter how many items are on the page.

5. **Careful with that mouse, Eugene.** The convention of placing two contradictory action buttons at the end of a web-based form has been around since the introduction of the World Wide Web. This has always confounded people who wondered why a "submit" button would be placed directly next to a "cancel," "start over," or other button that would immediately delete all their work. This is done less frequently in recent years and people have grown accustomed to being careful when choosing which of these

neighboring buttons to press, but I still shake my head every time I see this:

CLEAR ALL	CONTINUE

Reminds me of a buddy who put these fake buttons at the end of his web survey to make the issue even more obvious:

DELETE YOUR HARD DRIVE	SUBMIT SURVEY

Whether you are filling out a survey, an online reservation or any web-based form and you come across these contradictory adjacent choices, remind the company that it is no longer 1996 and that they should isolate their *Cancel, Back, Delete Form* and similar buttons from the *Submit* or *Continue* buttons.

Takeaway: After considering Lessons #1 through #14, compare your survey to this Lesson #15 checklist. By following all the lessons here in Part One, I guarantee you will gather accurate and meaningful information that genuinely represents your customers' opinions and your respondents will recognize that you went that extra mile to truly hear what they had to say.

Homework: POP QUIZ! What errors are committed in the following example survey item? Why do you think this would be an insulting question to some respondents and not provide accurate results? What would be a better way to phrase this item? Suggested answers are shown on page 83.

What is the highest level of education that you have achieved?
- ☐ *High School or less*
- ☐ *Some College*
- ☐ *Undergraduate degree*
- ☐ *Masters degree or higher*

PART THREE

ADVICE FOR FORMAT, PROCESS & INSTRUCTIONS

Lesson #16: Treat the survey as you would a "first date"

One of the most frequent questions I have been asked over the past 20 years is "what is the BEST number of questions to put on a survey?" My answer to this question is the same answer I give for many other survey construction concerns: <u>treat your survey like it is a first date</u>. Really. If you were going out on a date with someone for the first time, how would you want the conversation to go? The successful conversation would progress from topic to topic, asking relevant questions. You would show true interest by asking your date to clarify and expand on what was said, not monopolizing the conversation or asking personal details too quickly.

Contrast that with conversations you have had with your "date from hell," which are similar to how many surveys are worded. Consider these poor practices for a first date conversation (or for a survey):

1. Monopolize the conversation and pepper your date with a torrent of questions because hey, you never know, this might be the last time you see your date.

That is how many surveys are written: as if it is the last opportunity you will ever get to talk to your customers. I always advise organizations to focus their survey on one or two topics and save other topics for the NEXT survey. But no one wants their questions asked later; each department wants their questions asked now and the survey then turns into a 75-item monster. Instead, the survey should be a <u>conversation</u> where you ask a couple of questions and the respondent answers and then you close the loop by later explaining to the respondent how their feedback was used to make improvements. Follow this rule and you will have the opportunity for a <u>second</u> date and can ask more questions.

2. Wait until the end of the night to ask your date a series of personal questions.

Certain departments in an organization always demand to know the gender, race, age, job title and salary income of respondents, no matter how inappropriate or unrelated to the main survey topics. Even worse, these questions are usually found at the end of the survey ("so as not to skew the results" they say). At that point the respondent often wonders if her responses are now going to be filtered or interpreted in light of knowing she is a female Hispanic in a decision-making capacity earning $75,000-$99,999. If not able to opt-out of the demographic questions, many respondents simply end the date right there by closing their browser.

Is this what you would do on a first date: wait until the date has ended then blurt out "oh by the way, how old are you and how much money do you make and where do you work?" Not unless you wanted a second date! You would not be creepy on your first date so do not be creepy on your surveys either.

3. Ask your date a long series of multiple choice questions in rapid succession, not allowing your date to clarify answers.

That is what surveys often do. You may have wanted to rate the service somewhere between 4 and 5 stars but there is no option for this nor any comment boxes so you can better explain your thoughts. In the days of paper surveys, respondents went around this obstacle by filling in the margins or the back of the sheet to clarify their rationale for certain responses. But this option disappears in the online world if targeted comment boxes are not used. Do not just ask your date Yes/No questions like it is an interrogation. Give your date the opportunity to talk and tell you more!

4. **Make your date stammer and look silly by asking irrelevant or confusing questions**

Do not exasperate your date. If you should already know the answers to "what is your gender" or "degree earned," do not ask this on your survey – your date will know that you are not listening. Do not use complex branching in your surveys when a more straightforward approach will do. Do not ask survey questions that have nothing to do with the conversation topic or you will drive your date away.

Treating your customer like a first date with your survey helps fix so many errors. Doing so would nearly always eliminate these problems discussed in other lessons: (a) surveys created by committee where everyone wants to get their questions asked on the same survey; (b) mixing purposes; (c) having no focus or lack of purpose; (d) using inflexible vendor forms; (e) too much complexity; and (f) asking items for which you should know the answers.

Takeaway: Do not scare off your date! The survey conversation should not be an interrogation. Rather, focus on clear topics, of appropriate length, and allow the respondent to express opinions with plenty of comment boxes. If you were verbalizing these questions to the respondent in person, do you think your "date" would lose interest before the end?

Homework: Do you often stop filling out a survey because the questions are too pushy, irrelevant, personal, obvious, or lengthy? Is the survey maker being a good date? Overstaying their welcome? Or just being creepy?

Lesson #17: How to write the best instructions

How many surveys do you see in your inbox each month that lead off with these instructions?

> *"Please take 10 minutes to provide your honest feedback on this survey. It will help us improve our products and services." Or...*

> *"We value your opinion. Make your voice heard by completing this survey. It will take just 5 minutes."*

Experience has shown that you can significantly increase response rates by writing instructions that (1) are accurate in terms of time and effort required; and (2) do not turn off readers by using a generic (or false!) message.

When you submit your responses to an online survey, do you ever note how much time it took to complete? I do. In fact, of the more than 5,000 surveys I have created for organizations over the years, I intentionally sit down and fill out each one as if I am the recipient to gauge exactly how much time I am asking the respondent to sacrifice in order to provide their responses. I can assure you, it is rarely exactly 5 or 10 minutes! With just a little extra effort, you can provide instructions that will suggest to readers that you have put serious thought into your instructions:

> *"It should take between 6 ½ minutes and 9 minutes to complete this survey depending on how many comments you type because that was the range of time it took for members of our survey-making team to each complete this same survey."*

Say... now I <u>want</u> to complete this survey to see if I was in range! Well, perhaps not, but still it breaks out of the generic instructions mode used on 98% of surveys and lets the recipient know that you invested your own time as well.

In your instructions, a purpose such as "improving products and services" or "making your voice heard" is pointless. Of course that is the purpose, why else is the survey being administered? When I read that line, I am immediately annoyed because the survey maker clearly is putting in minimal effort. Worse yet, it tells me the survey maker does not know the real purpose of this survey nor how my responses will be used. You are asking me to give up my most valuable resource (my time) to help you. Since nearly 100% of all survey makers will never contact their customers to let them know what became of their responses, the instructions are your only opportunity to let your customer know what you will do. Try this instead:

"When you submit your responses, your typed (anonymous) comments for items #10 and #11 will be read by the Team Leader of each region. It is their responsibility to contact you by email within 10 days if your comments suggest a problem AND if you provided your contact information in the comment box. Your ratings to items #1-#9 will be averaged across all respondents and compared to the average rating from the previous month. If ratings have changed significantly, then we will identify the most frequently mentioned issues to learn what we did well or poorly this month."

Thoughtful instructions such as these let the survey-taker know there is a specific purpose and plan of action for these items and results, and an appreciation for the time invested to complete the survey.

Takeaway: If you want higher response rates and more meaningful responses, simply write instructions that clearly demonstrate: (1) you have invested thought into the process and (2) how the results will be used.

Homework: When you are asked to fill out a survey with the usual generic instructions, write back to the survey makers to say they will have to do better than re-use the "10 minutes" and "help improve our products and services" boilerplates in order for you to complete the survey. And in exchange for investing your time you at least need to know how your results will be used.

Lesson #18: How to prompt respondents to give meaningful and useful comments

As you know, the point of gathering feedback is to accurately hear what customers are saying, and then <u>act</u> on their responses. Respondent comments can provide useful insight, but people often provide ambiguous comments or none at all. Why is this? It is usually because the wording on the survey fails to sufficiently prompt respondents. Here is one example of poor technique:

Comments?

```
┌─────────────────────────────────────────────────────┐
│                                                     │
│                                                     │
│                                                     │
│                                                     │
└─────────────────────────────────────────────────────┘
```

This is the conversational equivalent of strangers passing on the path and one says "what's up?" or "how you doin'?" and the other responds "not much" or "good." Neither party has an expectation that anything substantive will be said. You should likewise expect just a word or two, if any at all, when you prompt respondents in this way.

This version is even worse:

Please comment here:

```
┌───────────────────────────────────────────┐
│                                           │
└───────────────────────────────────────────┘
```

This gives respondents the clear message that they are not to write more than 8 or 10 words as that is all the physical space you have allowed. Few respondents will bother to write outside the box or continue typing even though the characters are no longer visible. If any respondents <u>do</u> type a lengthy comment, this feedback is often given disproportionate weight, which is an error and a concern itself (i.e., survey makers who read a lengthy comment may focus on that issue and make it a higher priority than shorter comments).

The best practice is to write instructions that clarify (1) WHAT you want respondents to comment upon, (2) HOW they should write their comments, and (3) WHY their feedback is important (i.e., the Purpose, see Principle #1). For example:

> *"In order to better understand your ratings to the six questions shown above, please use the space below to describe a positive example of the service you received and an area of service that needs improvement. We will share your anonymous examples with all employees so they can discover what actions were noticed by our customers."*

In this example the WHAT is customer service, the HOW is to provide both a positive and constructive comment and the WHY is clearly explained. Avoid the ubiquitous catch-all: "Your feedback will be used to help us improve our services." Respondents are clearly aware of this – why else would they be receiving a survey? More specificity is needed to demonstrate that you are interested in hearing feedback. We will discuss this topic in more detail in a future volume of **THE SURVEY PLAYBOOK** series under Principle #7, "training respondents to provide better feedback."

Use the WHAT/HOW/WHY structure for each of the comment prompts in order to draw specific and useful feedback from respondents. To better target responses and make it easier on the analysis side, multiple comment sections, one for each major topic is best. For example, in a training evaluation, there could be one comment for each of these topics:
- instructor
- content
- course technology

For a restaurant survey, the comments could follow sections on:
- Service
- Food
- Atmosphere

Takeaway: Take the time to think of the what/how/why of each comment prompt. This exercise will often help focus the quantitative rating portion of your survey as well, as you discover the real purpose of asking for feedback.

Homework: Next time you receive a survey, look for the ubiquitous catch-all: "Your feedback will be used to help us improve our services" or for comment prompts that are the conversational equivalent of "how you doin'?" These practices indicate a survey maker who is not truly interested in your feedback.

Lesson #19: Mixing purposes

We have touched on this topic in many of the lessons, but it is such a painful error to make that it deserves its own lesson. The first Principle of Embedded Assessment™ is to focus your survey on a single purpose and to craft questions around that single purpose. If other purposes are important, then those items should be included in the next survey to be administered later. A sequence of "bitesize surveys" should be a conversation with your customers, each exchange helping to clarify one purpose or particular topic of interest (see Lesson #22).

But use of a single purpose is frequently ignored. Companies consider each survey to be their one and only shot at talking to their clients or customers so they want to be sure to pack in every question. Each time a survey is created or readied for launch, folks from every corner of the organization propose items to include.

Multi-purpose surveys are easy to spot as they contain far too many items, jump from topic to topic, and often look a bit schizophrenic with different sections written in different styles. The most common practice is to add a marketing purpose (e.g., ask for salary and demographics information) to the original purpose of the survey. These items always appear at the end of the survey (tricky, huh? We do not want respondents to see those questions until they finish their ratings, shhh...).

This type of multi-purpose survey often fails because it causes respondents to pause in midstream. Respondents who have to this point been providing their perceptions and ratings on one topic now arrive at the demographics section. Some will stop to consider the true purpose of the survey and think: "did I answer as a Hispanic female earning $75,000-$99,000?" "Will they treat my answers differently now that they know I am a 26-35 year old Caucasian male?" "Will they discount or emphasize my answers depending on how I am categorized?" Once respondents start questioning your motives, there is trouble.

Overlooked is the problem that multiple purposes cause on the analysis and interpretation side. Consider the reviews of a product you have read on a site like Amazon. A quick read of a few reviews can often help guide your decision because the reviews are focused on a single product. Compare that to reviews of hotels or restaurants on TripAdvisor. You have to read the reviews of many people to get a comprehensive feel for the hotel or restaurant because each review focuses on different aspects – one person comments only on the service, another on the price, and another on a heated discussion they had with the manager.

The same is true of your analysis of respondents' feedback. If you have a single purpose then most of the comments will be focused on that purpose and you can quickly gauge the situation by reading the comments (more like an Amazon review). If your survey is multi-purpose, then respondents will likely comment on some of the purposes but not others and you will have to read and synthesize many times the number of comments to identify the common problems (more like a TripAdvisor review). Of course you could just ignore the comments and act on the ratings but the point of the survey is to accurately learn what your customers think and that can only be done by reading their explanations and clarifications.

Takeaway: Have others re-read your survey. Can they determine what the single purpose of your survey is? Or does it look like a survey built by committee, asking far too many questions about too many topics?

Homework: Have you ever filled out a lengthy survey that looks like everyone in the organization had questions to ask you all at once? Did you take the time and interest to write comments at every opportunity or did you cherry-pick items that were of interest to you? Or give up before you finished?

Lesson #20: Too much complexity: Randomization, branching, skipping, and other unnecessary devices

Classic story: each year a learning organization assigns new employees to modify their annual Alumni Survey. Each year the survey grows in length and complexity because no one wants to remove any questions but there are new items that must be asked. After a few years the survey contains dozens of questions from multiple departments each using the survey for different purposes. The survey is then rewritten as four different web-based surveys, each one triggered based on the respondents' answer to the first question. Subsequent questions also trigger additional questions or different wordings of the same question. The survey is so lengthy and has so much complexity with all the branching and skipping involved that few alumni bother to fill it out (<6% response rate) and a shocking 40% of all respondents started the survey but did not finish. Even worse, the analysis involved to track and compare and match up the disparate questions takes the Insights Team more than six months to complete, at which point the next year's survey is on the horizon. The final report is of little use to administrators or any other stakeholders due to the small number of respondents. The exhausted Insights Team elects to cancel the next Alumni Survey while they retool it with even more complexity.

This true story is the result of many bad practices we have already discussed, including being a bad first date (Lesson #16), using stale items (Lesson #7), and mixing purposes (Lesson #19), as well as three additional harmful practices:

1. Psychobabble justification. In the story above, members of the Insights Team insisted that the survey provide each respondent with a "random" ordering of questions. They claimed that having the same ordering of items would "influence" their decisions and bring in "bias." When I ask them for empirical support for this practice, none ever surfaced, just vague references to "studies" (that did not exist) and to conventional wisdom (that was incorrect). When the words "accuracy," "bias" and "skew" are thrown around, watch out! - you are likely dealing with psychobabble. The randomization of questions on this survey was not justified. (A web-based <u>test</u>? Yes, ordering is important. But this customer survey? No.)

2. Too many stakeholders. In the creation and planning of surveys often there are simply too many cooks in the kitchen. The point of a survey is to have a single purpose with targeted and relevant questions so you can have a conversation with each respondent. When every department simply <u>must</u> have <u>all</u> their questions answered on this survey <u>now</u>, the effort will most certainly fail. The survey is supposed to be a conversation with your clients, not drowning them with every conceivable question in a one-time blast.

3. The team member who knows it all. I will never forget my conversations with one client where I offered to modify some awkwardly worded items and add a couple of obviously missing choices. The lead manager said "I will take you to the mat if you try to change anything on this survey!" And she was not kidding. Clearly I was dealing with the smartest marketing researcher on earth, but unfortunately for her team the messy survey they sent out was an uncontested failure with uninterpretable results and much finger pointing. There is no shame in asking for help – I have created and reviewed more than 5,000 surveys over the past 20 years yet I still rely on others to proof, contribute ideas, and challenge the wording and choices in my work.

> **Takeaway:** If your survey is chock full of branching, skipping, randomization, and other complexities you have multiple purposes and an unnecessarily long survey that will frustrate your respondents and yield poor results. Focus on what is important and save the other purposes for the NEXT survey. Seek input from others even if you think your final product is the best survey ever written!

Homework: Have you ever quit a survey before finishing due to the length, complexity, or ambiguity? It was likely the product of too many cooks in the kitchen or people justifying the complexity with psychobabble. Tell the survey maker to be more respectful of your time and simply ask the questions that are most important.

Lesson #21: Overuse of the NEXT button on surveys

Wow, this is frustrating. It is the most obvious tutorial I ever give but this problem never goes away. The practice of using the NEXT button in an online survey is almost universally despised, yet companies insist on including it thanks to the emergence of dozens of do-it-yourself online survey tools that include this feature, usually as the default. This annoying and bad survey practice continues to be further entrenched in our lives. We all know how this goes, right?

> **Q2. How satisfied are you with each of these 10 issues? Click NEXT for more questions...**
> *Oh no, not the NEXT button! Why can't they put all the questions on one page?*

> **Q12. Rate the quality of these 10 services. Click NEXT for more questions...**
> *Ugh, I wonder how long this survey is. I'm getting carpal tunnel!*

> **You are now 18% complete. Click NEXT for more questions...**
> *&%$!! I've had enough...* [Close browser]

This is an obvious case of "just because we <u>can</u> do something does not mean we <u>should</u> do it." We do not do this in the paper world, do we? - ask one question on the page and then have the respondent turn the page to see the next item? Why are we hiding the questions? I have personally created or modified thousands of surveys and evaluation forms across nearly every industry and not one of these surveys has included a NEXT button. Your surveys should not have one either.

One misguided reason used in its defense is that the ordering is important and you do not want respondents referring back or forward to other questions that might "influence" their decisions. This is psychobabble (see Lesson #20 for other examples).

All survey items should be visible to respondents at-a-glance. If the respondent has to click to another page to find more items, you have too many items. In a tightly constructed survey a respondent can see 15 to 18 questions on a desktop computer screen and that is plenty for a conversation. Respondents on a mobile device should be able to scroll through 15 to 18 items without having to click a NEXT button either. I understand that this advice has strong headwinds because do-it-yourself online survey tools often use BIG buttons and BIG checkmarks and BIG text so that your fingers get a workout scrolling down the page. Annoying your respondents in this way is one of the tradeoffs to consider when using DIY tools.

Each click of the NEXT button is a pause at which point the respondent can choose to quit the survey. As mentioned in previous lessons, you do not want respondents to pause but rather to become engaged in the smooth flow of the survey conversation and provide their feedback without interruption. Using the NEXT button not only irritates your customers but is guaranteed to provide you with sharply reduced response rates. Do not listen to misguided conventional wisdom: there is no empirical justification to "hide" questions. There is nothing to be gained and everything to be lost by using this poor practice.

Takeaway: There is no reason to ever use the NEXT button. It is good practice (and common courtesy) to allow your customers to see at-a-glance all the questions that you are asking. Choose another option if it is the default feature in your do-it-yourself survey tool. If there is no other option, then use another survey tool. Stop annoying your customers.

Homework: Rather than click the NEXT button a dozen times on a survey where they hide the number of questions being asked, close the survey and tell the survey maker to quit (Survey)monkeying around and use better practices that do not frustrate those they are asking for help.

SUGGESTED ANSWERS TO POP QUIZ

Did you forget about the Pop Quiz already? Or too busy skipping around that you missed it? Go back to page 62 before peeking at my answers!

- ✓ Be sure that your question allows for all reasonable responses
- ✓ Add a comment box so respondents can further explain their particular educational situation
- ✓ Make the categories distinct so your analysis is interpretable
- ✓ Consider how the answers will be analyzed and applied so that you do not annoy your respondents with categories that do not fit

Lesson #22: The bitesize survey

An excellent practice for engaging your customers and dramatically increasing response rate is the use of the bitesize survey or "microsurvey." We spoke earlier about the problems with lengthy surveys that contain multiple purposes, are overly complex, or use the NEXT button. The better practice is to administer a series of bitesize surveys to customers at regular intervals, just as you would in a conversation: you ask a couple of questions, your customer responds, and then you ask follow up questions. Each bitesize survey has a single purpose and no more than five clear questions with room for comments so participants can clarify their answers. The survey maker then uses the relevant Principles (e.g., Principle 5: closing the loop) and all the best practices we have discussed (e.g., Lesson #17: providing clear instructions) to ensure high response rate and engaged participants.

One of the best applications of this practice is in membership or alumni surveys. For example, in 2007 we resuscitated the membership efforts of an organization that had lost contact with many of their former members and who felt they no longer had a strong enough relationship to ask them for needed funding. We administered three bitesize surveys to their members over a six-month period, each with a specific purpose in this sequence:

Timing	Purpose of Survey	Sample conversation items
Week #1	Reconnect	confirm contact information
Week #12	Improvement	perceptions of organization
Week #24	Financial	solicit donations

By using this methodology the organization not only restored ties to more than 21,000 members but used member feedback to make noticeable improvements and generate 500% ROI in the form of gifts, up-sells and renewed memberships.

Empirical support for bitesize surveys can be found as early as Champagne (1998) where managers across 12 countries were given four short surveys over an eight week period to gather their feedback during a satellite-based training program. By quickly addressing the feedback and closing-the-loop, we obtained an average 86% response rate, manager satisfaction steadily increased over time and obstacles to the technology and learning were removed.

For those interested in the THEORY as to why bitesize surveys work or want to learn more about studies funded by the U.S. Department of Education to demonstrate this principle in action, see the **Further Reading** section below for suggested articles. However, the short story is that bitesize surveys work because they are consistent with psychological principles and encompass six of the *Nine Principles* of *Embedded Assessment*[TM].

Takeaway: Although the practice of bitesize surveys has solid empirical support and has been successfully used in Higher Education and training organizations for nearly 15 years, it has only recently gathered momentum in other industries. Your survey methodology is a CONVERSATION with customers and therefore you need to ask a little, stop and listen, and ask some more (see Lesson #16).

Homework: How many "conversations" do you have via surveys where an organization asks you a couple of questions and then follows up on your responses with another bitesize survey? Very few I bet. If you find examples of this good practice, please send my way!

Lesson #23: The folly of benchmarks: Failing to use <u>internal</u> benchmarks

This Lesson may turn-off a good portion of my readers – those who are convinced that they must have external "benchmarks" from their surveys in order to improve. These are the companies that:

- Use canned surveys from vendors who provide comparisons to "similar" companies, even though not all items on the survey are relevant to their organization;
- Use vendor surveys that promise benchmarking even though the survey does not solicit useful customer comments so you cannot interpret <u>why</u> customer scores are higher or lower this year;
- Pay exorbitant fees for benchmarking reports from vendors, even though they have the talent and expertise to analyze their own internal data.

It seems that the argument is over: most companies appear willing to sacrifice nearly everything for the promise of "meaningful benchmarks." They will annoy their employees and customers with irrelevant questions and lengthy surveys, spend enormous sums of money, and waste irretrievable employee time in order to learn whether they finished 5th or 9th this year in comparison to other companies of questionable similarity. In some cases the vendor will provide thoughts on how to improve relevant to other companies, but often the organization cannot determine why they fell short in certain areas.

What a waste. "But Doc, benchmarking and comparisons are important!" Yes, INTERNAL benchmarks have been repeatedly demonstrated to yield improvement. The most useful benchmarks are:

1. Compare your performance at Time 1 with your performance at Time 2.
2. Compare performance of one employee to another or one department to another.

3. Compare your performance against pre-set goals.
4. That's it. There is no #4.

Is there truly an organization exactly like yours? You may find two identical snowflakes before you find two identical organizations. So why do executives crave comparisons against other unique organizations within the same market when they can easily (and far less expensively) gather data on the three most useful internal benchmarks?

A story: Years ago, my University provided us faculty with overall ratings given by our students compared to those of the "national average" (benchmark). It did not matter that my ratings had improved from the prior term teaching the same course or that my scores were the second highest within my department. No, the benchmarks showed I was barely in the upper quartile among all professors within the vendor's sample, meaning 23% of professors at participating colleges had higher scores from their students.

But but but... I sputtered, are these professors teaching their courses for the first time or the 10th time? Are their students primarily non-majors like mine? Are they teaching to 10 students or 200 students in this course? Do they have access to the Internet and efficient teaching gadgets in the classroom? It did not matter. Even though my students, teaching methods, content, and classroom technology made my course unique, my student scores were rolled up and compared to all professors in the vendor's sample. So how do I improve compared to my "peers?" Who knows. That insight was not provided. The university was pleased that their huge financial investment yielded comparison data to determine our salaries but it did nothing to improve a single aspect of teaching or student learning term after term after term.

Does that sound like your organization? At the individual level none of us wants to be compared to some ambiguous group of people "similar" to us on a couple of characteristics. So why do executives insist on comparing their many individuals (aka, the organization) with others? It is wasteful and counter-productive. Unless your business is to make money <u>selling</u> canned surveys with benchmarking reports, of course.

Takeaway: Consider whether the information gained about external benchmarks is worth your organization's time and money. Did you learn specific insights applicable to your organization that have now been implemented and are showing strong ROI? If not, start using <u>internal</u> benchmarks to find the answers you need to improve?

Homework: Bring it on and tell me I am misguided! Would love to hear counter-examples, how external benchmarking was a financial win, and how benchmarking was the best way for your organization to improve and reach its unique goals.

Lesson #24: The folly of benchmarks: The inflexible vendor form

Classic story: each year a large learning organization delivers its web-based Satisfaction Survey to tens of thousands of students across the nation and uses the results in its marketing efforts. The survey is constructed by an external vendor and consists of more than 180 items in a fixed format. That is, even though many of the items are irrelevant or not of interest to the organization, none of the items can be removed because the vendor does not allow items to be removed. Students are instructed to skip items or to answer to the best of their ability if they do not understand the question or it is not applicable.

As you can easily predict, the survey frustrates respondents, yields low response rate, and generates ambiguous results. Respondents wonder why their organization wastes their time, asking them to wade through 180 items to decipher which ones are relevant. Analysts are unclear as to how students interpret these questions since some students leave many items blank and others choose a middle-of-the-road option for items that are not relevant. But this organization continues to pay the vendor an enormous amount each year for the same inflexible form delivering ambiguous results from fewer and fewer students because, well, because if they did not then they would not receive an annual report of ambiguous results to compare to last year's ambiguous results!

This true story is so sad because it encapsulates so many of the errors described in previous lessons - too many questions asked, irrelevant questions, ambiguous results, annoying your respondents, asking unfixable questions, and more. This organization also suffers from "benchmark envy." It does not matter that response rates are low, or that students are not giving their responses much thought, or that the results do not reflect the perceptions of their students. But it does matter that they have <u>numbers</u> now and can compare those numbers with similar organizations. Like the Emperor's New Clothes, the executives in the organization act on those meaningless results and promote these metrics in marketing campaigns, while those who are aware the numbers are meaningless keep quiet.

The same story is played out at many organizations where the standardized form and the promise of "benchmarks" overrides the best practices of creating questions and choices that are relevant and meaningful to your particular audience. Any vendor who is unwilling to modify their forms to include items and response scales that are a better fit for your purposes or make more sense to your respondents should not be hired.

This advice was hammered home by an executive of a regional accreditation agency who told those in Higher Education to stop using national comparisons and benchmarked surveys as support during the accreditation process. The agency was not convinced by colleges who pointed to their use of surveys by external vendors to demonstrate how they compared to others. The agency pointedly reminded them that they needed to measure important criteria within their own institutions (i.e., internal benchmarks, see Lesson #23) and make meaningful comparisons of their own progress.

Takeaway: Using a survey containing items that are irrelevant to your organization is a silly and wasteful practice. Arguing that it is justified because an external vendor submits the same questions to multiple organizations (to which it is also not relevant) is even sillier. This is not an accepted practice by colleges that need to demonstrate results and it should not be accepted within your organization either.

Homework: How often have you seen these surveys where you are forced to leave items blank or choose N/A because the questions are irrelevant? Often this is because the company is using an external vendor with a fixed survey. Tell the survey maker that this bad practice will not accurately reflect your true opinions and perceptions. And that they are wasting your time!

Lesson #25: Humor in Surveys

Here is an important topic that rarely gets much discussion. Why are surveys so humorless? Are we doing something so vital and critically important that we have to ask questions in such serious tones? We are not performing surgery here; we are having a conversation with our customers via a survey (although I am sure even surgeons tell jokes to one another over the operating table). Don't you open a conversation with your customers with some light talk and a couple of hardy har hars? Your surveys should follow the same practice.

Check your inbox and pull up the first survey you find (if it is late in the afternoon I am sure you already have several waiting!) Is there anything light-hearted about the questions or are they all business? Why? Are you more likely to respond to a survey that causes you to smile?

For years I have found it helpful to pepper most surveys with some humor. I have not put it to the empirical test but my experience and anecdotal evidence says that respondents are more engaged and we get higher response rates when we do the unexpected and give respondents a chuckle. More importantly, we get many insightful and funny responses in return, which helps build our relationships with customers. Here are a few examples that I have found to be effective with web-based surveys:

1. **The pop-up**. If the respondent chooses YES on a particular item then a bit of text appears: "That's great to hear!" or "Nice choice!" If respondent chooses NO on the same item then "Oh no!" or "Bummer" appears. My wife is a life-long Harley fan and rides a sweet Sportster, so it was a pleasure for me to advise on Harley-Davidson marketing surveys that successfully use this technique to draw respondents back into their shops to buy more gear.

2. **The instructions.** Lighten up the mood from the opening: "…Thank you for your time in completing this survey. It should take approximately 5 hours and 22 minutes. Just testing to see if you were reading these instructions. It should only take about 7 to 9 minutes to complete this survey…"

3. **The one-off.** The 3rd or 4th question of a survey is a good place to put an unrelated non-scored question that gives respondents an unexpected laugh. Best to make it obvious by having the final choice on that question something like "Hey, I don't like humor in my surveys" or "What has this question got to do with anything?" or "Ah, I see, you're just trying to lighten the mood here!"

4. **The confirmation page.** Once the survey is submitted leave your respondents with a smile. Write a humorous phrase or a personal message – the same sort of send-off you would give to any friend in a face-to-face conversation.

Of course not all surveys do well with humor. Be sure that the purpose and the audience are appropriate (e.g., you do not want respondents to be offended or in a bad mood while answering questions about employee satisfaction, see: http://www.humorthatworks.com/how-to/using-humor-to-create-fun-surveys).

Takeaway: Quit taking your surveys so seriously! A survey is supposed to be a proxy for an interview and a conversation between people. Use some humor and light-hearted words in your survey instructions and questions just as you would in a conversation with a friend. You may discover higher response rates and more eagerness to fill out your surveys in the future, as well as a few interesting retorts from respondents that help build your relationship.

Homework: I would love to see more uses of humor in surveys. Send examples whenever you find them!

PART FOUR

CONCLUSION AND APPLICATIONS

Nine Principles of Embedded Assessment™

WHY	1. Defining the Purpose and the Roles
WHAT	✓ Improving the Content
WHEN	3. Timing and Frequency
WHO	4. Participation and Ownership
HOW	5. Closing the Loop
	6. Use of Incentives
	7. Training the Respondents
	8. Reporting
WHERE	9. Mode of Delivery
RESULTS	Response Rate, Engagement, Loyalty, Success

CONCLUSION

Principle #2 of *Embedded Assessment*[TM] is to create clear, conversational and accurately designed content that produces interpretable and meaningful results while not annoying respondents. This Principle can improve every type of survey and evaluation form that exists. If you are responsible for CREATING surveys simply learn and apply the 25 Lessons of this volume to every survey you and your team constructs. If you are COMPLETING surveys, do not tolerate surveys that violate basic psychological principles. Instead, spread the word by telling the offending survey makers to apply the 25 Lessons.

Whether they are instructor or course evaluation forms, membership or alumni surveys, political polls, customer and product surveys, or any paper or online forms used to gather feedback from people, poorly constructed surveys will be here to annoy us forever unless we make a concerted effort to expose these bad practices. The remainder of this volume describes many of these Lessons as applied to case studies in Higher Education, Learning Organizations, and Industry.

Future volumes of **THE SURVEY PLAYBOOK** series will explain how to apply the other eight *PRINCIPLES* of *Embedded Assessment*[TM] to your surveys to substantially increase response rates, student engagement, and customer loyalty, as well as save time and reduce your current survey and evaluation costs.

Applications to Higher Education

The top 5 concerns about Course Evaluation
In 2012 and 2013, two national surveys of Higher Education were completed by faculty and administrators from nearly 500 U.S. colleges (Champagne, Nicholas, & Schepman, 2012, 2013). When asked for their concerns about the Course and Instructor evaluation processes at their institutions, the top answers were consistent across all three years:

1. Response Rate
Actually response rate would be the #1, #2, and #3 answer. Forty-eight percent of all respondents said this was a concern. As I have explained elsewhere and as we will discuss in length in Volume 2 of **THE SURVEY PLAYBOOK** series, the time and resources expended at most schools to increase response rates is just not justified. There are many proven (and free!) ways to encourage respondents (see especially Lessons #17, 21 and 22 in this volume).

2. Content
Issues about the reliability, validity, representativeness, ambiguity, clarity, and relevance of items were the second greatest concern. That is, "are we asking the right questions?" Surprisingly, a 2001 study found that the hundreds of unique items found on the course evaluation instruments of 78 colleges and universities could be reduced to just 16 criteria. That is, 94% of the 1875 items produced across all schools, many that were carefully crafted by individuals specifically for the needs of their students and faculty, all happen to fall within just 16 categories (e.g., instructor communication, fairness of grading). As I tell my clients, simply ask one question representing each of the 16 categories and you will have created an evaluation form that contains 94% of all reasonable criteria that can be asked.

3. Application of Results

What do faculty and administrators <u>do</u> with the results and how is this improving teaching and learning? How do we "close-the-loop" with students to let them know what action was taken based on their responses? Issues about the timeliness and access to reporting and the lack of interpretation of results were also concerns. Most vendors can produce comprehensive tables and graphs of results, some with more eye-candy than others, but few provide any meaningful interpretation results or guide users as to what to do with the results.

4. Unactionable Student Feedback

The concern is whether students are providing honest, accurate, and meaningful ratings and comments. Problems include not taking the process seriously, providing either no comments or vague, callous, and unhelpful comments, or making errors (e.g., evaluating the wrong instructor, accidentally flipping the response scale). Having reviewed the course evaluations from more than 700 schools, I know it is rare to find one that is error-free. Nearly all contain some level of ambiguity or incorporate poor practices, so this is indeed a justified concern. Applying the 25 lessons in this volume to your current evaluation form and processes, and applying Principle #7, Training the Respondents (to be discussed at length in Volume 2 of **THE SURVEY PLAYBOOK** series), will nearly eliminate this concern.

5. Mode of Evaluation

Decisions about whether to use mobile devices in the classroom to complete evaluations, obstacles with the current learning management system, transitions from paper to online, choice of external vendors, and existing problems with in-house evaluation are all concerns. The underlying reasons for these conversations (i.e., student access, cost, response rate) have not changed in 15 years (see Hmieleski & Champagne, 2000) but there are many best practices and a growing amount of empirical data now available to make good decisions. For example, an analysis of more than

400,000 student responses to course evaluations completed by computer, cell phone, and tablet found significant differences in response rate and number of comments typed depending on the device, but no difference in mean rating of instructor or course (Champagne 2013).

Applications to Learning Organizations

Earlier we described real-life applications of poor survey practices in Alumni surveys (Lesson #20) and Student Satisfaction surveys (Lesson #24). However, the most egregious survey practice in most organizations is the misuse of the Net Promoter Score. We have all seen this one many times, right?

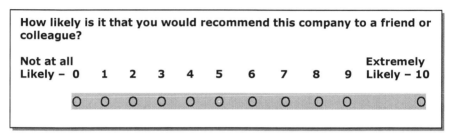

Use of the Net Promoter Score (NPS) to measure customer loyalty has long since morphed into a myriad of variations used to ask customers about the quality of experience with individual employees, such as this example:

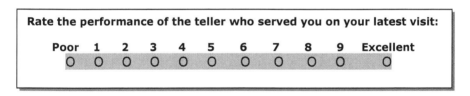

As I stated in Lesson #8, the use of this question itself is a favorite of mine because it can have many positive outcomes. However, it can only yield these outcomes when constructed correctly and analyzed correctly. As currently used, the NPS is flawed and the results misleading because it commits several of the errors described earlier including failing to define every anchor (Lesson #10) and creating ambiguous categories out of ordinal level data (Lesson #13).

Worse, the NPS ignores how humans make decisions, which is often devastating to employees whose salary, promotions and other rewards are based on these misguided results. Employees impacted by the NPS know that respondents MUST choose a 9 or a 10: the NPS calculation assumes that an 8 is <u>not</u> a recommendation and does not count as a positive score. In NPS lingo, a customer that rates the performance of a teller to be a 9 or a 10 is a "promoter" (positive score) but one who rates the same teller as a 7 or an 8 is "passive" and counts as a zero towards the score. Customers who rate the teller anywhere from zero to a 6 are labeled "detractors" (negative score) and all responses are lumped together as if they are equal (i.e., someone rating you a 6 is just as hurtful as those rating you a zero and both offset a 9 or 10 given by another customer).

Those who have read every lesson in this book should immediately recognize three errors already committed by the NPS by not allowing respondents to explain their ratings (Lesson #18), creating ambiguous categories out of ordinal level data (Lesson #13), and failing to define every anchor (Lesson #10). The NPS calculation goes even further into error and provides misleading results in all cases because it violates basic principles of psychological measurement, making false assumptions as to how people interpret scales. As you know, Rule #1 in Psychology is "people are different" and respondents have different perceptions as to what the undefined anchors mean. The NPS measure flatly rejects this commonsense rule and states that all people interpret an 8 on the scale exactly the same and this interpretation is that the respondent would not take time to recommend this company to others.

This misinterpretation is not only utterly false in theory but is rejected by overwhelming data and by data that anyone can collect and view for themselves. Having reviewed the NPS ratings and comments given by more than 900,000 people over a five year period, I have seen thousands of examples where individuals have provided a score of 7 or 8 and then typed comments to say how pleased and delighted and satisfied they were. This frustrates the company or the individual being rated because their response is, "gee, if you were so delighted why did you rate us an 8 instead of a 9?!" as if the respondent was supposed to understand the fatal flaws in the interpretation of the NPS.

To make things worse, companies than assign positive and negative scores to the categories, take the difference and turn it into a percentage, then view those percentages over time as if the contrived scores are now comparable. Essentially they take their customers' initial perceptions in the form of a number, then transpose that number multiple times at which point one cannot accurately interpret the customers' perceptions. For those keeping score, it looks like this:

Input **Ordinal** data –> transpose to **Categorical** data –> transpose again to **Interval** data = a hot mess

The solution is simple but rarely heeded. Rather than conduct multiple transpositions of your customers' initial perceptions, simply <u>keep the rating as is</u>. If someone rates your service as a 7 then it is a 7. If they rate it a 9 it is a 9. Calculate the means and this number can be compared across departments or over time. Of course it is still squishy in that we have not defined the anchors (see Lesson #10) but results will be interpretable if coupled with comments provided by the respondents.

A superior method is to use the scale discussed in Lesson #12. It has thoughtful descriptors for each anchor and the meaning of each anchor is clear and interpretable:

Would you recommend this company to a friend or colleague?
○ Definitely Yes
○ Probably Yes
○ Probably No
○ Definitely No

Each category is distinct. *Probably Yes* is categorically different than *Definitely Yes* or *Probably No*. Respondents that choose *Definitely Yes* or *Definitely No* their intent is crystal clear. Respondents can choose *Probably Yes* to indicate that they are not enthusiastic or do not plan to actively promote your business and that something has caused them to not choose *Definitely Yes*. Respondents can choose *Probably No* to not be a full rejection, that they have concerns or perhaps do not know enough information to recommend. A simple count of each category will tell your organization where you stand with your customers. Now that you can interpret your customers' perceptions, you can take meaningful action. The goal is then to get as many *Definitely Yes* as possible and then act on the comments provided to determine why customers lean toward or away from recommending your services.

Applications to Industry

For those who follow my survey reviews and advice at **MatthewChampagne.com** you know that I love cruising so it pains me to see cruise lines create poorly designed surveys that lead to bad decisions. Here is the "Ports-of-Call" survey I once received from Royal Caribbean, five months after our cruise. Using the lessons we have learned and from your own experience, see if you can identify the errors found in their invitational email:

Dear Valued Guest,
We are inviting a select group of guests to participate in a survey regarding the Ports of Call on a past cruise with ROYAL CARIBBEAN INTERNATIONAL. Your participation in this survey will help us to enhance existing itineraries and design future cruises that enrich your overall vacation experience. This survey will only take about 15-20 minutes. We hope you'll make your opinion count as your feedback is very important to us. Thank you in advance for your time and feedback.

Did you spot all the annoyances and errors? Here they are:

1. Asking for my feedback <u>five months</u> after the event. Who can recall specifics from five months ago? And how do those old memories compare to the reality at the time? And what of frequent cruisers who may have been on several cruises since that date and cannot recollect their experience of one port from another? Why did it take so long to ask these questions?

2. "Dear Valued Guest." I have only sailed with these guys a dozen times and they don't know my name yet? (see Lesson #2)

3. "This survey will only take about 15-20 minutes." Really? (see Lesson #17 to explain this error)

Now these instructions do a satisfactory job of explaining the purpose of the survey and how the results will be used (to enhance itineraries and design better future cruises), but the late arrival of this impersonal note makes me doubt their commitment. And I am certain no one will ever close-the-loop and let me know how my responses were used! Now let's move on to the survey itself. Here is the first block of questions:

Overall how would you rate the port of St. Thomas on each of the following?												
	Excellent	9	8	7	6	5	4	3	2	1	Poor	N/A
Cleanliness	O	O	O	O	O	O	O	O	O	O	O	O
Friendliness of locals	O	O	O	O	O	O	O	O	O	O	O	O
Safety	O	O	O	O	O	O	O	O	O	O	O	O
Range of things to do and see	O	O	O	O	O	O	O	O	O	O	O	O
Availability of things to do and see	O	O	O	O	O	O	O	O	O	O	O	O
Shuttle from ship to downtown	O	O	O	O	O	O	O	O	O	O	O	O
Taxi, bus, other transportation	O	O	O	O	O	O	O	O	O	O	O	O
Distance from ship to activities	O	O	O	O	O	O	O	O	O	O	O	O
Information provided on ports	O	O	O	O	O	O	O	O	O	O	O	O
Volume of people in port	O	O	O	O	O	O	O	O	O	O	O	O
Hours in port	O	O	O	O	O	O	O	O	O	O	O	O
Variety of tours/shore excursions	O	O	O	O	O	O	O	O	O	O	O	O

From the Lessons in this book, you should notice these errors:

4. The response scale has 9 points that are not anchored. Unacceptable. (See Lesson #10).

5. Can Royal Caribbean change the "friendliness of the locals?" The type of transportation found on the island? Move their port so it is closer to activities? Asking for my feedback on questions that you cannot change or do not intend to change is wasting my time (see Lesson #1)

6. Although we learned that N/A should not be presented as an option for every item (see Lesson #12) many respondents will choose N/A on this survey to mean "I forgot." Thus in the analysis it cannot be determined whether N/A means that the item was truly not applicable as in "not experienced" (e.g., I did not take a taxi or bus) or was experienced but forgotten. These are very different conclusions.

7. Was never asked the global question about satisfaction with this port, just asked the facets (see Lesson #7)

Other errors that are not obvious from this example include:

8. There are no comment boxes in this survey and no way to provide input and to explain or clarify my answers. This is absolutely unacceptable in any survey. Ever. How can improvement occur without specific feedback?

9. Turns out that the survey clocks in at 101 items, which absolutely violates Lesson #22 (using bitesize surveys) and Lesson #16 (treating your respondent as a first date).

10. Due to the incredible length, I had to hit the NEXT button many times (see Lesson #21)

11. This survey was absolutely humorless. How can an industry built on fun and a cruise line that prides itself on WOWing people offer such a dry, lengthy, boring survey? (see Lesson #25)

12. The survey uses a twisted version of the Net Promoter Score, taking a tool meant for customers to recommend services and morphing it into a rating of quality. A bad practice.

Overall, this survey violates 4 of the 9 Principles of *Embedded Assessment*^{TM} and therefore will have an artificially low response rate and far too much ambiguity of results to be useful. It also fails to follow at least 14 of the 25 lessons for Principle #2, the <u>WHAT</u> of creating good survey content. The results gathered by this survey will be misleading, failing to accurately capture the perceptions of the respondents and Royal Caribbean may then act on this misinformation.

Most egregious is violating Principle #3, the TIMING of the survey. It is important to note that the timing of this survey makes the results uninterpretable and misleading. That is, the survey asked me the same 12 questions shown above for four different ports. Of course, 5 months after the fact, the only facets about the port that I can recall with any specificity were those that went very badly ("ah yes, I remember how crowded that port was!" "That's right, I remember now how dirty that restroom was!"). Everything else that went well or as expected I rated somewhere in the middle of the scale because I cannot say something was *Excellent* from a hazy memory. I could have given accurate and useful answers 5 months ago but now my responses are mostly N/A (the only choice possible to indicate "I cannot recall") or negative because the survey has prompted me to think of areas of improvement for those specific facets. This survey should never have gone out in this format at this late date – Royal Caribbean will be best served by ignoring the results of this survey.

SUMMARY & FINAL ADVICE

Congratulations, you've found it: the secret page for the super-busy reader! If no time to read the 25 Lessons above, you can still significantly improve your surveys by adhering to these four rules:

Rule #1: Pretend you are the busy and important person who will be taking your survey.
Carefully read every word of your survey. Read the instructions. Read each item and compare to the response scale used. Are any items confusing, ambiguous or cause you frustration? Would you even want to fill out your own survey? So many problems can be eliminated by looking at your survey content from the perspective of your respondents.

Rule #2: Consider every choice that could be made for each item and determine if that response can be interpreted in only one way.
If people choose N/A is it clear what that means or could that response mean several things (see the Royal Caribbean example above)? Do you know what they are trying to say if they choose *Agree* or *Disagree*? Or if they choose a *2* or a *4*? After the data is collected is not the time to learn that you forgot to include reasonable choices or that you have lost data due to the way the items or response scale was structured.

Rule #3: Think of how the results will be analyzed and applied ("Begin with the end in mind" as Covey would say).
Are you asking respondents for feedback on things you can't change anyway? Will 90% of responses for an item be skewed to the same answer? If so, how will you address this? Is there so much complexity in the survey that the analysis will be too difficult to perform? Taking time to imagine different results scenarios will force you to re-think your survey content and structure so that you can logically and efficiently apply the results.

Rule #4: Most important of all, be a good first date!
Your survey is a CONVERSATION with your audience. Be considerate of their time, ask just enough clear and relevant questions to get the conversation rolling, and allow them to respond before you ask more questions. If you pummel your date with a mammoth list of complex, confusing, and unrelated questions because you believe it to be the one and only chance to talk to your customer it will be a self-fulfilling prophecy. Yes, thanks to this poorly-constructed survey, that WAS the last conversation you ever had with that customer.

FURTHER READING
("FURTHUR reading" for all you Merry Pranksters)

THE SURVEY PLAYBOOK series continues with Volume 2: Closing-the-loop, training your respondents, and providing the best types of incentives to increase response rate and engage your audience.

Join our community of survey experts and survey practitioners, enroll in some courses and learn much more at: **MatthewChampagne.com**

NEED IMMEDIATE HELP?

No time to read a book because you need to create that survey or evaluation form today? Need another pair of eyes to review your survey before it launches tomorrow? Write me and I'll help as quickly as possible! **champagne@EmbeddedAssessments.com**

KEEP THE CONVERSATION GOING!

Let's stay in touch. I can be found on most social media platforms as "The Evaluation Guy" or "Doc Champagne" but best places to connect are:

Facebook.com/DocChampagne

LinkedIn.com/in/MattChampagne

ABOUT THE AUTHOR

Dr. Matthew Champagne has influenced the practice of evaluation and assessment in higher education and learning organizations for over 20 years. As an instructor, Senior Research Fellow, evaluator, consultant, and serial entrepreneur, Dr. Champagne has created and implemented innovative feedback technologies in hundreds of organizations across every industry.

His current missions are to (1) rid the world of poorly created surveys that annoy customers and misinform organizations, and (2) educate the world on creating surveys that increase response rates, gather timely and meaningful feedback, and rapidly improve customer service and retention.

When not researching, writing, presenting or consulting, "Doc" can usually be found on a cruise ship with his wife and three children, on stage with his rock band, or scuba diving in the Caribbean.

REFERENCES

Champagne, M.V. (2013). Student use of mobile devices in course evaluation: A longitudinal study. In K. Morrison & T. Johnson (Eds.), Educational Research and Evaluation: An International Journal on Theory and Practice, 19:7, 636-646. London: Routledge.

Champagne, M. V. (1998). Dynamic evaluation of distance education courses. Proceedings of the 14th annual conference on Distance Teaching and Learning, 14, 89-96.

Champagne, M.V., Nicholas, J. P., & Schepman, S. B. (2012). Report on the 11th annual survey on course evaluation in higher education. (*Embedded Assessment* Series #28).

Champagne, M.V., Nicholas, J. P., & Schepman, S. B. (2013). Report on the 12th annual survey on course evaluation in higher education. (*Embedded Assessment* Series #32).

Hmieleski, K. M., & Champagne, M. V. (2000). Plugging in to course evaluation. Archived at: **technologysource.org/article/plugging_in_to_course_evaluation/** (*Embedded Assessment* Series #9).

ACKNOWLEDGEMENTS

My sincere gratitude to all those who helped bring this first volume to life:

To **Greg Cosgrove** for his cover art and design, book promotion, and countless hours running the business side of Embedded Assessments while I hid out to write this book.

To **Dana Champagne** for her editing and feedback on the many drafts of this volume.

To **Stephen Konya** for his review, creative input and encouragement to turn my blogs and videos into a book.

To **Beth Bumgarner** for her reviews and advice throughout the writing process.

To Advisory Board members **Ron Davis** and **Todd Schnick** for their time, encouragement and direction. Learn more about their work:
Ron Davis at www.sivadsolutions.com
Todd Schnick at www.intrepid-llc.com

To the entrepreneurs and gurus who helped me connect the dots with their advice and examples:

David Meerman Scott, marketing & sales strategist extraordinaire whose every post is a must read: www.davidmeermanscott.com

Wayne Breitbarth, the best and only source for LinkedIn strategy and advice at www.powerformula.net

Tim Grahl and his team for their extraordinarily helpful advice for authors found at www.timgrahl.com

To my **many clients and colleagues** whose questions and ideas are an ongoing source of learning.

NOTES

NOTES

NOTES

Made in the USA
Lexington, KY
25 August 2019